Acknowledge the WONDER

Cover Art:
The painting *Chandrabhaga* by Nicholas Roerich is reproduced by permission of the Nicholas Roerich Museum which holds copyright to this work of art

Acknowledge the WONDER

Harmony with the Natural

Frances Wosmek

This publication made possible with the assistance of the Kern Foundation

The Theosophical Publishing House
Wheaton, Ill. U.S.A.
Madras, India/London, England

A Quest original. First Edition 1988

The Theosophical Publishing House
306 West Geneva Road
Wheaton, IL 60187

A publication of the Theosophical Publishing House, a department of the Theosophical Society in America.

Library of Congress Cataloging in Publication Data

Wosmek, Frances.
Acknowledge the wonder.
(A Quest book)
"A Quest original."
Bibliography: p.
Includes index.
1. Philosophy of nature. 2. Spirituality. I. Wosmek, Frances. I. Title.
BD581.W67 1988 113 87-40521
ISBN 0-8356-0628-7 (pbk.)

Printed in the United States of America

Contents

Foreword vii
Chapter 1
Waves of Change 1
Chapter 2
Children of the Light 19
Chapter 3
The New Reality 35
Chapter 4
Harmony with the Natural 47
Chapter 5
Hear the Music—See the Dance 65
Chapter 6
Between Me and Thee 79
Chapter 7
In the Eye of the Beholder 95
Chapter 8
Authorized Truth 109
Chapter 9
The Language of the Birds 123
Chapter 10
Stir a Flower and Trouble a Star 135
Bibliography 147

Foreword

If this book proves to be unclassifiable, then I have achieved my purpose. Like buttercups in a spring marsh, we have all bloomed into individual being, inseparable from all that surrounds us. Threads of meaning bind us to every other thing and each other. Severing too many of those threads results in the death of the spirit.

Education strays from reality when it divides its knowledge into separate compartments without due regard to the connections between them.

It is my earnest hope that these few wholly inadequate and limited pages will help remind someone who may have forgotten that miracles abound everywhere—every day. And, in the words of Edgar D. Mitchell, Apollo 14 astronaut:

> There are no unnatural or supernatural phenomena, only very large gaps in our knowledge of what is natural. . . .We should strive to fill those gaps of ignorance.

1
Waves of Change

Infants in their first year, it would appear, are not so much engaged in learning as forgetting. There is something profoundly wise in that intense, studied gaze from the cradle. Going one step further, it is easy to be convinced by their expressions that what they are seeing astonishes them no end. But then, looked upon with fresh eyes and an unprogrammed brain, this must indeed seem a most astonishing universe.

However, in time, and with normal development, those infants will learn to adjust to the "ordinary" without astonishment or wonder. They will learn to look without seeing, react without feeling, and hear only what they want to hear. And that will take a lot of forgetting those things which they were born knowing inherently and instinctively. The fact that the cool, self-possessed giants who people their world have forgotten so much may be what surprises those little newcomers most of all.

Reaching back to the beginning of one's own memory often reveals that the impressions which have been strong enough to survive through time were those too "ordinary" for any of the grown-ups present to have noticed at all.

Etched in my own memory, with far greater clarity than any event before or for a long time after, is the image of a glowing, golden globe throbbing with life and color, shooting lights of astonishing intensity and beauty. The golden globe was a brass knob on my mother's old four-poster, shining in the lamp-light. I was three and a half. I know I was three and a half because the event was one that went down in our family history as memorable—the birth of my only brother. However, the faces of my mother, the new baby, and my father proudly displaying them have faded to fuzzy blobs which would probably have vanished years ago except for their association with that spectacular fireworks of shooting sparks from the brass knob on the bedpost.

That little child—undistracted by what was being pointed out as the big event worthy of celebration—could stand transfixed by a display of enormous beauty that everyone else had long before learned to take for granted. She had not yet learned the rules. If the birth of a baby brother came second to a dancing brass knob, she did not think to question it. She felt no guilt at all—only a pleasure so intense that it would last for more than half a century.

How much of that ability to be aware, to see directly and clearly, is left, if any? We are programmed to survive, produce, and consume. We are feared as competitors and solicited as allies. So much of what we say, think, do, or feel has been adopted from second-hand, time-worn impressions that have become stereotypes, as effortless and tasteless as a TV dinner.

It is easy to see in looking back, that life and the living of it is quite different from what it was when we began. If we are any age at all, we can clearly see that everything has speeded up considerably. The merry-go-round whirls faster and faster. By the time it becomes apparent that we are getting nowhere, the neck-breaking speed at which we appear to be hurtling through time makes getting off or changing direction seem altogether too risky for most of us. How did we manage to get ourselves caught up on this treadmill energized by so much pain and effort, and often to so little avail and apparent meaning? But, even more importantly, is there any hope of change for the better?

Distinctly different world views have successively engaged the imagination of us in the West, determining our behavior as well as what we think of ourselves. The ancient Greeks had not yet separated themselves from nature. Reason, not experiment or observation, provided their best means of discovery. By the sixteenth century the humanistic movement had altered that view in seeing humanity as separate and apart from nature. This objective view of reality led naturally to experimentation and observation, and to inductive science.

Christianity, on this point, was not in conflict. It, too, saw humans as apart from nature and, furthermore, saw God as offering them a privileged place in the scheme of things, though with the Creator in full charge of the mechanics, which they believed to be infinitely beyond human understanding by any means other than faith. ''Let there be''—and there *was,* a divine gift asking nothing more than gratitude, humility, and cooperation in return. The meteoric rise of modern science was the most wrenching of all changes, putting the very reins of command into the hands of humans, and filling their minds with intoxicating promises of domination over the kingdom of which they suddenly saw themselves lord and heir.

Those old beliefs and values which had confirmed and supported our ancestors for centuries were all but banished to gather dust in the mental attics. In their stead, the collective allegiance, trust, and even a kind of awed, narcissistic worship were offered to the precocious, powerful young god of Science. The physical region of reality, which could be experimentally proven and manipulated, enticed the best minds and engaged the full attention of almost everyone. And why not? Being in control seemed undeniably to prove humans capable of nearly all the miracles theretofore attributed to God. Or, so it appeared, just as long as the view could be kept narrow enough, and as selectively focused on substantiality as a well directed lasar beam. All those annoying, cloudy, uncontrollable subjective inconsistencies such as life, consciousness, and self-awareness, together with all their accompanying meanings and values, failing to follow the rules, were offhandedly categorized as incidentals or, at best, as by-products of matter.

Their reality was equated with dreams, illusions, and the rest of the invisibles resisting provability, or otherwise slipping through the net of the physical senses—or extensions thereof.

Unfortunately, a host of unforeseen problems accompanied that spectacular human rise to power. What had not been taken into account was the "ego-mania" that was to come, hand in hand, with the new sense of limitless power. The universe is a cooperative system, if there ever was one. The countless small self-interests of its tiny earth inhabitants were not a force significant enough to make much impact on the whole, but they did tend to clutter and disrupt the natural harmony between humans, their neighbors, and their environment. Only when disturbances of the long-taken-for-granted earth harmony showed signs of becoming alarmingly inharmonious, was its importance fully realized. The humans' very existence, it began to seem certain, depended on it.

Quite suddenly, inhabitants of the earth found themselves beset with seemingly insurmountable problems of environment, population, and economics. To make matters worse, even individuals seemed to be losing the personal sense of purpose and worth that had relied on a belief in some power transcending themselves. Insecurity breeds distrust, and so humanity began to see itself as perpetually in danger of attack—from the enemy, disease, poverty, or its own self-destructive attitudes. So people armed themselves "on the ready" with weapons, drugs, and exerted all efforts toward an excessive accumulation of wealth and power to ensure a steadily growing oversupply. They crowded into urban settings, seeking out an increasing number of superficial relationships to prevent the necessity of ever having to confront their own deepest selves.

The possibilities for realizing humanity's dreams have never been greater. Communication satellites have made possible a community of the world. News can be received from anywhere instantly. We have become a people of "omnipresent" information. Through hi-tech computerization we are able to plan, predict, and understand better than ever before. Since the space missions, we are learning to look upon Earth as one planet rather than a collection of separate continents or nations. Most of our forefathers' fantasies have become realities or, at least, reasonable possibilities. Plans are already in the making for an extension of ourselves in mind-blowing space colonies.

But the rewards of science have not lived up to their promise in many of the expected ways. It was not until our planet had become satiated with the most advanced methods of communication ever conceived that we discovered we had very little of anything worthwhile to communicate. Sophisticated computers are clogged with the wheeling and dealing of self-serving entrepreneurs. Like a snake swallowing its own tail, television feeds on itself, encouraging ever more consumption which, in turn, demands more production, and all to no end but an increase of waste and surplus. Luxurious automobiles, which would have been the envy of past emperors, are jammed in traffic, lined up at fast food windows, or on their way to the mall. From every possible direction, through every available medium, from the very beginning of reason, each one of us is being conditioned never to be satisfied with enough. It has become nearly everyone's dream to win a lottery and so, in gluttonous self-indulgence, wallow in nonessentials forever.

So many things and so much power have failed to satisfy as replacements for the less spectacular, slower moving, old-time harmony with the natural, and we have suffered through failing our responsibilities to earth and neighbors.

We need to go back to the old maps of the human spirit left to us by our wisest ancestors, comparing them with the latest, stunning discoveries of our physicists, noting the similarities, and seeing how each one reinforces the other. We need to reevaluate our position to make sure we are not discarding something valuable in our enthusiasm for change. The dazzling successes concerned with the "hows" and "whats" of our reality have all but obscured the more subtle but equally important "why?" and "to what end?" What we sense to be the best of ourselves aches with the need to know.

Prowling back in time via one of the oldest known pieces of literature, *The Rig-Veda* of India, can be a surprising revelation to those who believe the "new" ideas to be entirely new. Blow the dust of the ages off the idea of "agni" and see what you find—"A glowing golden dust," ''wine of lightning in the cells of the body,'' the ''solar fire'' in matter, ''builder of forms.''

> Oh, Son of Energy [the Rig-Veda sings] this is the Force-Consciousness. This is a heat, a flame, at the very level whatever we catch it. When we concentrate in our mind, we discover the subtle heat of the mental energy or mental Agni; when we concentrate in our heart or in our emotions, we discover the subtle heat of the Life-Energy or vital Agni; when we plunge into our soul we know the subtle heat of the soul or psychic Agni. There is but one Agni from top to bottom, a single stream of Consciousness-Force or Consciousness-Energy or Consciousness-heat which clothes itself in variable intensities according to the level. And there is the fundamental Agni or material Agni which is the ultimate stage of the energy of consciousness before its conversion or condensation in Matter. This is the place of the passage from one to the other. (V111.84.4)

The *Rig-Veda* is a collection of ancient hymns from an age before the intellectual philosophies of the West. Its conception is lost in antiquity. But the words ring strangely familiar to the modern mind.

Modern science is reaffirming some of those most ancient of views. Little by little, it is reaching back (or advancing ahead) toward the ground of all being, and rediscovering, on a higher intellectual rather than emotional level, that the individual is not an ''island unto himself.'' Everywhere is confirmation that we swim in a sea of influences that inexplicably join all into one system of universal reality.

There even seems, inherent in every human soul, the merest ghost of some far-off unity, originally known, when I was ALL and ALL was I. There is a poignancy of separation that makes itself felt behind our most revealing experiences, touching the edge of memory like a fading dream:

> There's a certain slant of light,
> Winter afternoons...
> That oppresses, like the heft
> of Cathedral tunes....
>
> Emily Dickenson

History reveals that human cultures have always developed intense ways of perceiving and expressing the single reality and their relation to it. The very word "religion" means "reconnection," suggesting a basic need of humanity to reclaim that which they sense they have lost. The god image comes naturally to the image-making mind of an individual drawn to the center. The concept of that which, dependably and even lovingly, guides one's development through time into ever more complex and meaningful patterns has been envisioned most clearly as a "superbeing," an enlarged and idealized version of the human.

In one way or another, that image has remained one of the most persistent archetypes of all nations, all cultures. Though its influence and emphasis may rise and fall, it has never completely disappeared, and is notable for rising up from a seemingly dormant state, stronger than ever. The mind's need for connectedness with the ground of its being has not diminished over those long and arduous millenniums of its struggle to reach the light.

Just as our image of the universe, the Earth, and our place in relation to each of them has changed with the illumination of new knowledge, so too must the image of our inherited "God" be adjusted to complement the new vision. It may be that the physicist is in a better position to reveal the secret nature of reality than the contemporary churchman. It has even been suggested that physics might *be* God. However, matching human-size images with the grandeur of the universe in its totality—particularly within the tight limits of a language designed more for pragmatic use than abstract thought—must always fall far short of the mark.

It may even be that God, as a conceptualized being, has lost relevance in the light of new understanding:

> The projection of God is a fundamentally aggressive act. We create an authority with a Divine Will separate from ourselves; this Will must be imposed on our own will and, in the cruder forms of theism, on the wills of others. Then, having created duality by inventing God, we must dissolve it again by mystical contemplation. It might be faster and clearer not to have made this projection to begin with.
>
> *The Light from Different Windows*
> Stephen T. Butterfield

The physicist has already stepped over the line of the material and entered the mysterious quantum world of the atom. This is a gateway to a better understanding of what lies beyond the world of the senses, which has until now remained outside the bounds of the reasoning intellect. The wonder, the miracle, and the mystery of the old religions are all there, enhanced and elaborated, only this time involving the whole of our natural selves and the world equally, without prejudice, without exception or exclusion.

The past century has seen some of the most rapid and bewildering changes in the history of mankind. But the feeling of union and communion with a reality beyond and more permanent than one's individual self is still as much a need of the human spirit as it ever was. It is a natural hunger seeking natural nourishment. And this time, the "god" that is beginning to rise, phoenix-like, from the ashes of the old is as natural as the earth itself. We are extending our knowledge to include it. There is no longer any need to resort to the supernatural to discover the miraculous.

However, the "Way" for any individual to establish identity in relation to the whole is no longer as clear as it once was. It is no longer possible for anyone to catch onto the coattails of someone else's vision, and glide through life without the effort of ever having to think for oneself.

The public power of most religions has declined to not much more than a memory. Yet, at the same time, multiplying choices spread out before the seeker in bewildering array—denomination split from denomination, exotic Eastern religions, gurus, Humanists, Born Agains, as well as the steady pull of pure materialism preached and practiced by some of our most eminent leaders. It is hardly any wonder so many turn their backs on them all, hoping the gnawing emptiness in their insides will go away.

Sincere seekers for a meaningful ground to stand on in today's jungle of alternatives need to be prepared to carry their own luggage. They will need a good supply of common sense, a little healthy skepticism, and the ability to stand their ground if the way of others does not seem to be their way. It is not important whether seekers choose to do their exploring and discovering inside a place of worship or outside one, their learning inside or outside the walls of academia. Some naturally prefer the greater flexibility of a "loner." Others need the support of a group. Just as each of us is unique, so should be the path of our connectedness.

For me the way opened naturally. Parents and circumstances conspired to gift me with an enviably uncomplicated beginning. My early memory was not imprinted with an indelible image of the Great Reality as an expanded ego. My simple understanding was not confused by difficult esoteric ideas—or, even worse, by distorted esoteric ideas. So, what I sensed for myself, in my raw, childish innocence, never needed to change in essence, only deepen with understanding.

I was born into an isolated corner of northern

Minnesota. In my early years, I had few friends—except for the furred, feathered, and four-footed kind. My part in nature seemed as natural as breathing.

I was never lonely. I knew, with a certainty that would be hard to explain, that I was not alone or apart. I sensed something beautiful just behind all that was, something that seemed as interested in me as I was in it, something even more supportive than my very dependable parents.

Strangely, there had been no direct religious influence from anywhere to touch off my budding metaphysics. My mother, an old-time Methodist, and my father, product of generations of devout Catholics, delicately compromised their differences by avoiding the subject altogether. Fortunately, relatives and churches of either faith were too far away to disrupt my parents' neutrality or my freedom to move as the spirit directed.

There was one thing my parents had in common. Each was equally God-fearing in its most literal sense. I was very sure, right from the start, that I did not want their stern, judgmental God forever looking over my shoulder. What I had discovered all by myself was a beautiful Something, and I was not about to trade it away for anyone's God. So I kept it a secret. I leaned increasingly toward it, just as it seemed to lean increasingly toward me.

Later on, I thought I would find communion with others who felt as I did in some church or other. Invariably, I was disillusioned. I found nothing to equal what I already had. Perhaps I missed it—or failed to see it. But there was more to what I had in mind than putting on a Sunday hat and going through a ritual that seemed to have little meaning for anyone. And why only on Sunday? What I had found operated equally well on any day of the week.

In some cases it even seemed to me that the church served as little other than a hotbed for self-righteousness and narrow-mindedness. And so, a little sadly, I turned away from them all and continued on my way.

I read voraciously and indiscriminately for a number of years, hoping for a glimpse of that elusive Something which seemed so real to me and, yet, apparently, not so to a lot of others. I read books of every faith, every persuasion, from every culture and every time. Gradually, I began to cull out what seemed to me intuitively to strike a wrong note. Somewhere along the way, I picked up what I sensed was a thread of truth. I followed that thread from book to book, lecture to lecture, and to an occasional fellow traveler at about the same stage and sincerity as I.

I found at least a trace of what I was looking for in each of the faiths, though in many instances it had become so encrusted with self-interest and politics that it would have been easy to miss. But I was convinced that in almost every case it had been there, alive and healthy, in the beginning.

I picked up the same thread in books of science, particularly physics, and even in books about art, and poetry—lots of poetry. I heard it in music. I smelled it in the fragrance of flowers. I saw it in the eyes of babies—babies of all races and species. I saw it, alive and bright, in the faces of some of the very old, even though their material selves were fast fading away. I saw it everywhere in nature. In fact, I could find a little of it almost anywhere if I looked hard enough. And strangely, excitingly, it was the same truth.

There have been rare and wonderful moments when the light has shone unwaveringly bright for me, illuminating everything to a clarity that melted the bounds of separation. If my faith in it had ever needed confirming, it would have been definitively confirmed during those times. But even in the long stretches between those shining moments, knowing It was there has guided me through the hard pulls, and seen to it that I came out a step higher each time. I even sensed an "unseen hand" (or a nudge) when it was needed, when I had reached my own conscious limits. The contact was made first in some deep, bright place within myself (or, maybe, it was "out there," or even both). Only after that would I become aware of changes, inside and out. Magical changes. I accomplished things, when the need was great enough, that I could never have had the strength or ability to accomplish without it.

That which has brought beauty and meaning to my life is beyond form, words, or labels. It could be described equally well in any number of ways—or none. It does not matter. It is very real to me. *That* matters.

Acknowledge the Wonder

It seems my childhood thoughts and feelings, or others very like them, might have been universally experienced by many of those who acquainted themselves early enough with the earth in their own way. For instance, American Indians spent their days in a kind of free association with nature, much as I did:

> . . . But very early in life the child began to realize that wisdom was all about and everywhere and that there were many things to know. There was no such thing as emptiness in the world. Even in the sky there were no vacant places. Everywhere there was life, visible and invisible, and every object gave us a great interest to life. Even without human companionship one was never alone. The world teemed with life and wisdom, there was no complete solitude for the Lakota.
>
> Luther Standing Bear, Lakota Sioux
> *Land of the Spotted Eagle*

2
Children of the Light

In this charming little village by the ocean where I live, it is now well past the time of autumnal equinox. Already the trees are stripped bare of leaves, save a few "hangers-on" clinging to the fantasy of sweeping off their twigs in a lusty twirl of snowflakes.

Canadian geese have been V-ing past my window, off to their version of Miami Beach, for quite some time now. But a few of the birds, like the yellow leaves, prefer to hang on until the last minute, hoping against chilly hope that summer might yet change its mind, surprising everyone with a sudden, unexpected about-face.

Yesterday morning anyone listening (and few were) would have been intrigued (as I was) by the combined chatter coming from dozens of small throats that swelled from the bare branches of a naked old elm. There were more starlings than most of us could have comfortably imagined. Each was having its best top-of-the-lungs all-out say. Being heard seemed important, yet no one appeared to be listening (with the exception of myself).

Being the human I am, I found myself seriously limited to the language of my species. But by combining my share of the standard reasoning and imaginative capabilities of my kind, I had something to draw on in putting myself inside the skull of a starling (a commendable feat for a five-foot-seven-incher).

"There's a long, long trek ahead of me," I clearly imagined the small birdling think. "The way stretches over a lot of territory unfamiliar to me. I will be leaving behind my favorite backyards and all my favorite crumb-sprinklers. I know I will meet up with many unknown dangers—storms, hawks, and even many things I lack the imagination to fear. Though my closest friends and family will be winging along by my side, even a few of us would be helpless against all those terrors without the support of others—a lot of others, a flock that blackens the sky. Only together will there be a chance for us or, at least, for some of us."

I nodded dryly, feather-tongued. "But why. . . ," I silently asked from that word-empty void between languages, "why do you waste all that energy screeching for hours on end instead of conserving it for your coming ordeal?"

The starling smiled. (Whatever it was in starling, it would have been a smile in human.) "We 'screech'," it replied patiently, "as you so crudely put it, each in our own individual way. When we begin to hear those separate voices as one lovely song of recognition, we are ready to chance the long and dangerous journey. Only then have we no fear of getting lost or losing touch with our friends. You see, together we are each more than just a starling. We are *starling,* one body and one voice. No journey is too long or hard for one so strong and wise."

Most scientists engaged in searching out the secrets of the universe are carefully screened and highly educated intellectuals. However, it is safe to speculate that only a few of them have had more than the most superficial brush with poetry. Yet, those of us who listen with an intellectual ear, then process the information through "right brain" understanding, are convinced more and more that what we are hearing from the new science is a good deal closer to poetry than it is to prose.

Matter is a condensation of energy or light, they are saying—frozen, interconnected patterns of light. Now matter, if anything, is basic. Matter is where we humans, as well as all the rest of our biological cousins, took our first real stand. It is the point from which we embarked on that long and dangerous evolutionary journey through time. You might say, then, that we are "children of the light," and if that does not qualify as poetry, then nothing does.

In the beginning, and for a long time after, in that tedious upward climb toward knowing ourselves, we were obedient children. Nature had the firm upper hand. We moved as we were moved, here and there, like checkers on a board. No dissension. Nature made mistakes, but corrected them in her own good time without any help from us. Only after the way had been cleared for the thinking brain and individual self-consciousness to appear did the floodgates to potential conflict between the evolving and the evolved open, once and for all.

It was probably inevitable that the new little human creature—with such an enormous potential for imagination, capacity for error, and limited access to the whole knowledge—should come to grips, sooner or later, with the Original Plan. By giving this precocious young upstart a free will, intellectual possibilities, a memory into the past, and vision into the future, evolution in essence offered, too, a corporate share in the Grand Plan—a vote, as it were, in the planning itself.

That little neophyte, with the oversized ego only matched by a huge propensity for good and evil, has not done too badly. Multitudes of us are here to attest to that fact. Enough of the choices must have been correct, or nearly so—or at least not too drastically off course—or so many of us would never have survived this long. Not that mistakes have not been made, because plenty of them have. But nature, so far, has been generous and forgiving, compensating for our errors, or allowing the time and room for us to rectify them for ourselves. Always enough of us have been on hand and ready to fill in for those who had the bad fortune to be lost in one of the more serious blunders. An oak tree scatters a great many acorns. It is enough if only a few of them survive the squirrels, the weather, and all the other natural hazards, and go on to become bigger and better oak trees.

In only the past few decades or so, all that seems to have changed. There is a dis-ease and foreboding in place of that old relaxed, shoulder-shrugging assurance of alternate options in the aftermath of a wrong decision. The choices needing to be made by our generation and the next may be the most critical and urgent of any in human history. This time we see little room for error. The scope and intensity of destruction that would follow any number of wrong choices could eliminate all further possibility of choice. Mother Nature, if she had a breath to hold, would be holding it as she suffered over *her* decision to entrust so much to so small and vulnerable a creature as the human individual.

For better or worse, most of the choices that will determine our fate henceforth will be ours to make. There can be no retreating back to a benevolent nature that was ready to risk anything to ensure our survival. We have left the nest. We must learn to fly, or fall to the ground.

It is a huge responsibility. The consequences of a major blunder could be as severe for us as they were for the failed dinosaur or the dodo bird. Or, if we turn away from making any decision at all, we might sink back into evolutionary decline, having proved our species incapable of handling or upholding its short-lived top-ranking position, possibly locked into learned life functions with all the robot-like, mechanized efficiency of a bee, an ant, or a termite. We would probably not be missed if we were to step down from our high post. Any vacancy left by our falling back would almost certainly be instantly taken over by some other alert line of being anxious to prove its adaptibility and endurance.

Fortunately, there are other, better ways still open if enough of us have the foresight to recognize them, then insist on the attitudes and action to bring them about. Humanity has proved itself resourceful to the extreme whenever the necessity has arisen with sufficient urgency. On that point rests our hope and any future claim to remaining in full power as evolution's leading edge.

New and increasingly urgent emphasis is being directed toward the all-pervasive holism in nature, and in that "nature" we are being included. Self-indulgent thoughts of ourselves as privileged guests of the universe—free to exploit its many treasures to satisfy our needs and greeds, devoid of any responsibility—are coming to an end. The new view sees us as part of one harmonious linking of cosmic events. As Hippocrates, wise before his time, cried out to a mostly deaf wilderness, "There is one common flow, one common breathing, all things are in sympathy."

The ancient Chinese expressed their understanding of the pattern of wholeness centuries ago. They had no words, and needed none, to describe what the West was to call "the laws of nature." They saw reality as continuous, fluid change. They called it *li,* which translates to something like "dynamic pattern."

This dynamic pattern was distinguished by the cyclical direction of its ceaseless motion, reflected variously in the cycles found everywhere throughout nature. The concept was provided thought structure by indicating two polar opposites, each containing a little of the other. These two, called the *Yin* and the *Yang,* are well known in the West today. Symbolically, the Yang represented those qualities attributed to masculinity, qualities of strength, aggression, and power. Conversely, the Yin had to do with the feminine—nurturing, caring, subjective qualities.

These two poles were in no way separate, but opposite extremes of a single whole, serving to set the limits for cycles of change. The Yin, having reached its climax of power, was seen to retreat in favor of the Yang, and vice versa. All manifestation was generated by the dynamic interplay between these two archetypal poles. Nothing could be just Yang, nor could it be just Yin, but always an oscillation between the two. As such, both poles were granted perfect equality with no positive or negative values attached to either one. Rather, a balance between the two created a positive "good" or harmonious effect. An imbalance, on the other hand, represented the opposite, a negative, "bad," or evil effect.

Our place in modern times, so strongly materialistic and egocentric, could be no more classic example of an age dominated by the Yang. It may have reached the climax of its power, or nearly so. If it has, then, according to the old Chinese thought, a gradual turnaround might be expected, the Yang's decline in favor of the Yin.

Looking back over recent years, it would seem

that such a change may already be in the making. Efforts toward the equal rights of women have resulted in a marked flow of the feminine (subjective, or Yin) point of view into the work place and other places of power. On the other hand, men are being encouraged to develop the Yin side of their natures through more conscious fathering, and a tempering of the aggressive aspects of their behavior. Cooperating with, rather than exploiting, earth has become an important issue. Some of the evils due to an overbalance of the Yang in our society might be expected gradually to subside.

The universe is not a creation the same as a painting or a piece of sculpture, a one-time "thing" completed and final the minute the artist lays down his brushes or the sculptor his tools. From the very beginning, the universe has evolved as a process, continually changing and unfolding its inherent possibilities. It is a unified field of relationships, not a collection of things. All forms of the objective world, including ourselves, are abstracted from the deeper order, a kind of energetic web with enfolded patterns of expression probabilities.

> All things by mortal power
> Near and far
> Hiddenly
> to each other linked are,
> That thou canst not stir a flower
> Without troubling a star.
>
> Francis Thompson
> "The Mistress of Vision"

It seems that there is no such thing as "pure" matter or "pure" energy, but that matter is energy "mattering," and energy is matter "energizing." Each extreme contains within it the potential for its opposite, just as the Chinese said centuries ago.

We humans are not so special as we were once led to believe. We are integral parts of the whole, firmly implanted in the system, our roots deep in time. We exist in a sea of natural forces, within and without, forces binding each to himself and each to everyone and everything else in organized patterns, hierarchically arranged, each part of a larger, more complex whole. We are part of a web creating a continuous network of influences, totalling the all-inclusive whole reality. We are bound to the earth by gravity. The moon is bound to the Earth, the Earth to the sun, the sun to the galaxy, and on—and on. We would be hard put to find a point of separation.

In the beginning, the whole was indisputedly without difference. Science declares, with convincing evidence, that an actual beginning (at least in this cycle of existence) did occur about eighteen billion years ago, bringing space and time simultaneously into being with the celebrated Big Bang. But something other than the explosive force was needed promptly to direct the chaos into becoming an orderly universe where almost everything runs harmoniously and "on time."

The characteristic order of the universe unfolded naturally in spite of the second law of thermodynamics, which broadly stated describes the tendency of a gradual, inexorable slipping of everything into increasing disorder (entropy)—a law operative just as much then as it is now. But order was bound to occur. Natural reactions between components inherent in the system had foreordained its success.

Physicists recognize four fundamental forces that direct the natural order. They are the electromagnetic, the weak nuclear, the strong nuclear, and gravity. The first three are strong and local, and are important in the subatomic world, having to do with the very smallest units of energy.

Gravity, though billions and billions of times weaker than the other three, distinguishes itself by being the most all-pervasive and cosmic of them all. Gravity not only unites but separates as well. Objects responding to a strong gravitational pull move away from other weaker attractions. Gravity is essentially behind much of the order of the galaxies, having shaped them, and even yet continues to uphold their motions as well as motions between the bodies within them.

Though in Newtonian physics gravity is thought of as a force, Einstein perceived it in a different way. To him gravity meant a stretching and distorting of space and time in the presence of mass. In this conception space is curved around large bodies including our sun. As a result, planets moving in their orbits are following the path of least resistance.

The mathematics of both views turns out to be

the same, but the two views suggest different ways of understanding space and time.

In the very beginning, due to the extraordinarily high temperatures created by the Big Bang, the four fundamental forces did not exist separately, but as one. A unity like that would have been a state of zero entropy or a perfect symmetry—albeit a sterile one.

Something remarkable happened with the rapidly falling temperatures following that dramatic thrust into being. The cooling separated the perfect unity into imperfect fragments and, with the creation of mass, gravity came into being and organized the primal stuff into galaxies, then eventually, into individual starforms. It was gravity, too, that compressed those aspiring young stars into the complexity that led to the full range of chemical elements. Already, within that original stardust was the potential (possibly even the necessity) of you and me, along with every other aspect of our familiar twentieth-century world.

The "would-be-but-failed" perfectionists among us should gain heart by realizing that, on the whole, perfection gets one nowhere. It seems our very existence is due to the creation of imperfection from that first, pure, untarnished perfection!

Living beings appear to mirror the larger spectrum of reality in forming clusters like the stars. They too seem drawn together by natural forces, both subjective and objective. Love can bind two units into a significant relationship just as much as can gravity. Atoms pattern themselves into specific forms or creations. Humans are inclined to do the same. Since the Stone Age, individuals have been gathering in cohesive units of family, tribe, settlement, and eventually city, state, and nation. Within those conglomorates, countless other smaller groups come together to accommodate some certain set of common needs or interests, forces which also draw and bind individuals together. "A man without a country" exemplifies one of the greatest terrors an individual can face—to be shunned from the society of one's peers.

The first need of a human infant, or almost any baby of a certain complexity, is a bonding with its mother, or some other vital connection with a representative from the reality to which he or she aspires acceptance. Without that loving, outstretched welcoming hand, the child misses forever the opportunity of feeling included in his or her world and society, and to which any infant so rightfully belongs.

"I" become meaningful only in relation to "you." Reality, in order to exist in a normal way for anyone, must present itself as a dialogue. There are few hermits, and those there are have lost their identity to the degree that they believe themselves cast adrift from their fellow beings.

Entombing one's self within a small, personal world can only result in the death of the spirit. Reaching out to the mysteries of other-ones and other-wheres, paradoxically, means reaching to the innermost parts of oneself.

No two persons' points of view nor their interpretations of what they see are the same. All of us create unique personal worlds within the infinite possibilities of our senses' reach. We create time by dividing our short lives into convenient and manageable portions, measured in relation to celestial movements of the Earth and moon. We create our space out of distances within which we can easily move, putting ourselves always at the center. We take our world circle with us wherever we go, the radius determined by the range of our senses. Our circle may impose on others' or others' may impose on ours, enhancing and enlarging our view or confusing it.

More than likely, we will never achieve the satisfaction of knowing a single "why" of our becoming, any more than our limited, earthbound brain could ever meaningfully grasp a clear purpose behind the vastness of the universe. Any answer would necessarily include understanding the why of the why, and that would be a little like looking into one's own eyes.

It should be enough just to realize the wonder of our awareness, the ability to look back to our beginnings as no other being (so far as we know) has been able to do. It should be enough to know that we carry our banner in the front ranks of a journey that began with the beginning of time. It should fill us with reverence and awe just to know that the elements of our makeup are the same as those of the stars. What in the "supernatural" could equal the miracle of hydrogen 1, simplest of the elements, having grandfathered us all—or that even you and I were implicit in that celebration to top all celebrations, the Big Bang?

Good luck on your way, little starling! Though each of us represents the road not taken by the other, we began as one somewhere—sometime long ago—in the heart of a star.

3
The New Reality

The sky is a pale, luminous pewter grey. The fading sun filters through the haze, highlighting the gleaming landscape with a transparent amethyst wash. Lavendar-winged gulls glide over the water to their homes on the islands. The entire world seems to quiver in a single, harmonious, amethyst-violet cosmic chord. The effect lasts only an instant, but that instant is a glimpse over the wall. For hardly longer than a held breath, the mask has slipped.

After such an experience of abrupt awakening, the viewer is often left with a feeling of overwhelming helplessness and loss, a sense that nothing in this material world is any more permanent than the fleeting glimpse of an amethyst evening. Suddenly, the old way of looking at things comes up for questioning. What do we mean by "real" if everything in our experience is illusory or, at best, temporal?

The past few decades have seen startling things happen to the old reality concepts. The full impact is yet to come. When some of the steadily advancing stream of revolutionary ideas creating wonder and amazement (and a little uneasiness) in the advanced sciences begins to trickle down to a general understanding and practical application, the lives of all of us will undergo a fundamental change.

Until only recently, Western perceptions of what was "real" had been based on the view of a random, mechanical universe, the whole of which amounted to the sum of its parts. Such a whole was thought to be best understood and dealt with by an intensive study of each of the parts, a combination of which would be a fair representation of the totality. In such a system, educators felt justified in instructing their students to dissect a live frog and observe its beating heart in a jar of alcohol, intending that the children would appreciate and understand a living animal. A person was believed to be a detached observer, somehow apart from and superior to the rest of nature. Conflicts could be put straight if only the right set of rules could be found, and since every effect had a cause, anything should be predictable, if only a full set of causes could be known.

Education, science, medicine, and almost everything else in society were structured according to those premises. Considering humanity's advantage over the rest of the earth and its creatures, such a view was an open invitation to human manipulation of any of the parts that were potentially advantageous to its own interests.

The new view is far more complex, challenging, and mysterious, indicating a unified whole with an underlying web of interrelatedness and interdependence not yet totally understood.

The new physics emerged from two great revolutions of thought, the quantum theory concerned with the behavior of atomic and subatomic matter, and Einstein's theory having to do with space, time, and motion.

"Anyone who is not shocked by quantum theory has not understood it," declared Niels Bohr, a frontrunner in untangling some of the bizarre implications of the new discoveries. Physicists tread the new ground cautiously, well aware that they are often trespassing on some of the sacred territory of ancient mystics, their thought running parallel to old and holy concepts. A diligent scientist, accustomed to hard and fast rules and solid facts, has no small difficulty in coming to terms with such oddities as events without causes, ghostly images that spring into reality upon observation, and atoms reacting according to the expectations of the observer. To its human observers the subatomic world seems chaotic and confusing, haunted by uncertainty and unpredictability.

It was unsettling to discover that an observer in a conscious act of attention was not as distinct from the observed as logic would seem to imply. Being observers themselves, physicists were taken aback to discover that even their own enlightened views fell short of total objectivity. Yet they discovered that there could be no such thing as a wholly objective view. Something of the viewer's instruments and self always perturbs the situation in some way, significantly influencing the results.

Those explorers of the unknown were equally unprepared to accept the wave-particle mystery lurking right at the heart of ordinary physical reality. In the well-known experiment designed to determine the exact qualities belonging to earth's most basic constituents, matter and energy, light was chosen to represent energy, and electrons were selected to stand for matter. Everyone was confident that light (energy) would prove to be a wave phenomenon (continuous) and that matter (electrons) would demonstrate atomic or particulate (discontinuous) qualities.

Not so at all. Surprisingly, each displayed contradictory aspects, both of continuity and discontinuity (though not at the same time). The irrefutable fact was there. Light traveled as a wave, and interacted as a particle. Somehow a qualitative leap had been made into a contradictory aspect. The physicists were forced to conclude that common sense might prove an undependable aid in the world of the atom.

No one has ever seen an atom and, most likely, no one ever will. It is far too insubstantial to be caught by the human eye. In our time, its image has been changed from the first crude, probing model that scientists attempted imaginatively to construct in explaining it to themselves. In those early days, it was thought that atoms were simply particles held together by forces of energy, somewhat akin to the sun and its planets which are kept in formation by gravity. The model fit neatly with the then prevailing view of separate "things" and "events."

Scientists tell us that atoms are mostly empty space, proportionately somewhat like a golf ball orbiting a football in a space the size of St. Peter's cathedral. The electron whirls around its nucleus at a rate estimated to be 6,570 thousand million revolutions per second, so fast that it is virtually everywhere at once, creating the grand illusion of solid matter.

Einstein's now-famous equation $E = mc^2$ confirmed that mass and energy are interchangeable. Energy, it said, is equivalent to the mass, multiplied by the speed of light squared. From that equation, it is easy to see that the tiniest scrap of matter is capable of converting to a stupendous amount of pure energy. A scant square inch of earth is all that it would take to send a train speeding on its way for thousands of miles. This same energy, powerful beyond belief, is identical with that locked in the atoms of every material thing of our everyday world—including our very flesh and bones.

It seems that science has stumbled upon an underlying unity, the ground from which all being springs, and a "wholeness" that cannot be diminished by space or time, or as the words of Charles Williams, the poet put it, "Separation without separateness, reality without rift."

David Bohm, prominent theoretical physicist and former associate of Einstein, presents a holographic picture of the universe in which the complete pattern of the whole is implicit in every part. He sees the overall pattern as enfolded and merged in even the very smallest parts.

At the quantum level, parts (waves, particles) relate to the environment that surrounds them in intimate ways more suggestive of organs within a living body than parts of a constructed, mechanical device.

In the light of these new views, the individuals and their place in the whole have been dramatically transformed. Western thought has traditionally concentrated on objects or on parts of objects—atoms, molecules, and cells—in its efforts to understand the phenomenon of life. However, the search was frustrated by the abrupt and capricious vanishing of "object-ness" into a mere wave of energy that slipped from material grasp with no more trace of its being than a passing thought.

Increasingly, attention is shifting to a comprehensive view, in which "aliveness" is seen to be a quality of the planet in its entirety. Looked at in this way, life becomes a continuum in which individuals exist only as perturbations in the total energy flow. Various energies flow to and radiate from each of us, bearing sustenance for our needs, and allowing us to contribute to the needs of others. For example, the nitrogen needed by each one of us has first been processed in countless ways by countless other organisms while, at the same time, their necessities are being supplied through processing by appropriate neighboring organisms, in a constant, invisible flow. The intricate web of supply and demand maintains a steady balance that serves to support the material existence of all of its parts.

An individual in the life system might be compared to a vortex in a stream of flowing water. The vortex has no material reality in itself, and would not exist if the stream stopped flowing. It retains its identity even though molecules of the water are constantly changing. The vortex, as such, is simply a pattern existing temporarily, or for as long as the stream of on-going water sustains it.

From such a view, one could conclude that individuals do not exist per se in the material world at all. Their true ''reality'' retreats back into the shadowy world of patterns such as Jung's archetypal images or Rupert Sheldrake's morphogenetic fields, all seeming more at home with old spiritual traditions than with conventional concepts of biology.

Ideas of this kind may be more satisfying if simply felt rather than intellectually analyzed, in much the same way one comprehends and appreciates music or some other art. But even a glimpse of their truth cannot help but change significantly the way we think of ourselves and others.

Understanding wholeness lifts the issue of ecological balance from an aesthetic vision and concern to a new and desperate urgency. If the life system is deflected too much off course by short-sighted and egoistic intervention, it is possible that humans may lose the stability they require to exist at all in the material world.

So many new and startling jolts to conventional thought leave today's confused layman almost no familiar ground to stand on. Even the concept of objective, linear time is being seriously questioned by modern physics. The resultant definition appears bizarre, undependable, and even mystical to most of us—the past interchangeable with the future, a beginning and end to time, and clocks that slow down as they travel in space—all ideas becoming commonplace today.

Einstein was responsible for transforming the comfortable allotment of hours and minutes, doled out by neat ticks of the clock, to a mysterious "no-thing" that is elastic and can be stretched or shrunk by motion. Most of us are familiar with the notion of a theoretical twin who was blasted off into space in a rocket at close to the speed of light. The earthbound twin waited ten long years for his sibling to return, but on that great day the earthbound one was amazed to discover that the traveler had aged just one year, while the earthbound one was ten years older. The high speed of the rocket had allowed the adventurer to experience ten years of Earth time in just one, as measured by their different time scales.

The barrier for such time-gymnastics is, of course, the speed of light. Nothing, in theory, can go any faster than that. If it could, it would be a matter of turning time inside out—finishing the race before it began, so to speak.

However, such an event is not likely to happen in actual fact. Even though the speed of present-day rockets is impressive, they would need to travel much faster in order to create a significant time warp. Precision, atomic clocks on board rockets show only a hardly measurable acceleration of time.

For each individual time seems to move dependably along within his or her own personal time scale without distortion. But there is distortion in relation to someone else's time scale—if that person happens to be traveling at a speed incredibly greater or less than one's own. Time, as the reliable absolute it was once believed to be, seems to have abandoned us forever. To "flow with the years" has all but lost its meaning. It seems time does not flow. The sense of its moving is simply the mind's way of perceiving it.

Paul Davies in his book *God and the New Physics* has this to say about time:

> The physicist...does not regard time as a sequence of events which *happen*. Instead, all of past and future are simply *there*, and time extends in either direction from any given moment in much the same way as space stretches away from any particular place. In fact, the comparison is more than an analogy, for space and time become inextricably interwoven in the theory of relativity, united into what physicists call *spacetime*.

Implications of these new ideas permeate into the smallest aspect of our individual lives, and are as far-reaching as the end of time. The old reality as independently existing "chunks" of matter, living or dead, had seemed relatively safe and controllable to humans as they stepped back from nature in an egoistical attempt to appraise what was in it for themselves. The new view destroys that confidence in their power to control, and demands another more intimate and cooperative relationship with those things from which they are separated by no such definite bounds as they had thought.

Reality—not as bits and pieces or building blocks, but pattern, process, and interrelatedness—has a mind-like, and even some would say, spiritual quality. In such a universe there is no sharp division between the animate and inanimate, the living and the dead, but a gradual flow from one to the other—by degrees, not by definition.

Humans throughout their thinking history have always clung to believing that it was the "within" of themselves where their finest treasures lay. It now seems that each "within" is conjoined with the within of everything and everyone else, expanding everyone's essential being to include the universe. Going deeply enough into the heart of anything, one's self equally with the atom, reveals that same incomprehensible glimmer of a common spirit.

...the reasonable assumption
of the possible existence
of a total comprehension

of the integrated significance—
of the meaning—
of all experiences.

Buckminster Fuller
Ever Rethinking
the Lord's Prayer

4
Harmony with the Natural

When a steady breeze blows over the water, it creates a continuous roll of whitecaps that rise and break with hypnotic regularity. They are small waves. Several offshore islands protect my favorite beach from the main brunt of the open ocean. Except in hurricanes or northeasters, these are mild and gentle, as waves go.

Most shore creatures appear to be so much a part of the color and motion of the sea that it is difficult to imagine them separately. Sandpipers, for instance. Sometimes clouds of them appear, seemingly from nowhere. In one body they drop, light as air, close to the water's edge. They roll on a blur of tiny, stick-legs at the precise speed of the receding wave. They lift exactly in time for the next wave to break. They are gathering insects, one can see, with the quick, scooping dips of their little heads.

I find them at work most often when the sand is pink with the last rays of the setting sun. It would not surprise me to hear that they came from the same mythical, uncharted land as do the leprechauns and gnomes, since they vanish as quickly as they come, without a trace. Where they spend their days is a mystery—at least, to me.

As much as anything I know, sandpipers live and act in perfect harmony with each other and their environment. All their movements seem synchronized by one central controlling power, and that power moves with the same naturalness and ease as the wind.

I watch them, perhaps a little enviously, but I never see *them* watching *me*. If I move too quickly, I trigger an escape response, but I never catch them looking back over their shoulders with any kind of curiosity whatsoever. Obviously, I am so divorced from their reality that, for them, I simply do not exist. Only the bulk of me, as with a falling tree or a stroke of lightning, instinctively reminds them of a situation that might prove dangerous, and ought to be given a wide berth.

The sandpiper and I have arrived at where we are by the same means, albeit different routes. We have evolved out of nature to express, each in a different way, the one life force that supports us both. But somewhere along the line has come a difference of relation to our common source. The sandpiper, in its unthinking innocence, harmoniously upholds its one small ecological niche with no untoward notions of interfering with that which already is.

On the other hand, we humans have developed—along with the opposable thumb, complicated brain, and adaptive genius—the desire and ability to shape what we see according to our own best interests. More often than not, we are thoughtless or ignorant of the best interests of the earth itself, and of all those other living forms which laid claim to the planet aeons before we late-comers arrived.

It took longer than it should for us to realize that our long-term interests were best served by attending to the best interests of all, inseparable and interdependent as they are turning out to be. To have overlooked this important fact for so long has left this confused generation (but not the sandpiper) heir to a variety of mental and bodily ills that the American Indian would have diagnosed as "loss of centeredness."

It is too late for us to regain the lost innocence of a sandpiper, spontaneous harmony based on its natural instinct; and it still remains to be seen if we can measure up to a complex, thoughtful harmony through conscious action motivated by an expanded state of ecological awareness.

Appreciation for the earth, so long taken for granted, took a significant step forward when the first astronauts floated free of terra firma, far enough away from their home planet to bring back an objective view. Their accounts were glowing, describing a suspended sphere, periwinkle blue and emerald green, dazzling as an emperor's crown jewel set against a black velvet void. There is nothing else like it for light years on any side, they assured us. Everything else within distance to compare is indescribably bleak and barren, very hot or very cold. For all intents and purposes, planet Earth is one of a kind, and well worth whatever it takes to save it.

Russell Schweichart, the first man to walk in space without an umbilical, returned from the adventure with stars in his eyes. He had this to say of looking back on the homeland from a moon's distance away:

> . . . And a little later on your friend goes out to the moon. . . . He looks back and . . . sees the Earth, not as something big where he can see the beautiful details, but . . . Earth as a small thing. . . . And the contrast between the bright blue and white Christmas tree ornament and the black sky, that infinite universe, really comes through . . . the size of it, the significance. . . . It is so small and so fragile . . . such a precious little spot, that little blue and white thing . . . everything that means anything to you . . . all of history and music and poetry and art and death and birth and love, tears, joy, games, all of it on that little spot . . . that you can cover with your thumb. And you realize, from that perspective, that you've changed . . . there's something new . . . the relationship is no longer what it was. . . .''

In the heyday of the Greeks, scientists and theologians alike looked upon Earth as an awesome and mysterious phenomenon, mostly beyond human understanding. In the face of such shared abysmal ignorance, but with respect for its obvious power and influence, scientific and theologic visions tended to merge. It was reassuring to think of the mysteries as being understood and controlled by appropriate gods who could serve, when necessary, as medians between themselves and the powers that were. In the same sense, the Greeks named the goddess of their Mother Earth ''Gaia,'' helping to bring it a little closer to human understanding. Thinking of their planet as allied with a personality, even though of a vastly higher order than themselves, at least provided some common link between them.

This feeling of relatedness between humans and their home-earth was put on hold for centuries in the West, while earthlings developed and tested their own powers to subdue and control the planet, as it had apparently so long subdued and controlled them. In spite of countless spectacular successes, there have been enough dismal and important failures to give pause for a reexamination of the grounds of our position. Some of the old ideas of our not-so-ignorant-as-we-thought ancestors look quite different when viewed from the higher level of knowledge that we now command.

The Gaia hypothesis as postulated by scientists James Lovelock and Lynn Margulis stirred considerable interest by its contention that ''the entire range of living matter on Earth, from whales to viruses, and from oats to algae, could be regarded as constituting a single living entity, capable of manipulating the Earth's atmosphere to suit its overall needs and endowed with faculties and power far beyond those of its constituent parts.''

Scientists are seldom willing to embrace such a mystical view, or one that seems to threaten their solemn guardianship of the facts. But they do continue to gather evidence confirming the mysterious, self-regulatory quality of planet Earth. Though the elements of its makeup are remarkably close to those of Mars and Venus, Earth has displayed the capacity to maintain its delicate balance of life-supporting conditions over a very long period of time, something which its sister planets seem to have been unable to do. Life in the form we know it prospers only within a narrow temperature range, and needs air rich in oxygen, water, protection from lethal cosmic rays, and other specific conditions. Earth, tiny in a dynamic and ever-changing universe, has managed it just right for millions and millions of years. Even though cosmic accidents have sometimes devastated its balance, in the end the planet has always succeeded in setting things right again without any help from anyone.

Sixty-five million years ago, impact with an asteroid is believed to have occurred, with destruction severe enough to have caused extinction of the dinosaurs. It is conjectured that the cloud of dust and debris raised by that disaster obliterated the sun, creating freezing conditions on Earth, enough to have made it hostile to some forms of life for a considerable time. Nonetheless, when the dust cleared Gaia, it would seem, brushed herself off, repopulated herself with a new variety of appropriate animals and plants—all the while proceeding serenely on her regular orbit.

The hypothesis of Gaia declares that not one of us on Earth can be alien to the rest or to the whole. We all have our own uniquely specified roles to play in this gigantic, dynamic, interdependent system. We are a cooperative of smaller systems grouped into the unity of one complex whole, with consequences that would be impossible or inconceivable to any one without the others.

From this point of view, the planet is more than just our home. It is an extension of ourselves. Whatever benefits it, benefits us. Those things that weaken its effectiveness weaken ours as well. If we eliminate a species, we have eliminated one important aspect of our own experience.

We humans are the eyes and ears of Gaia. It is through us that she sees and hears the wonders of her creation. It is through the human mind that she becomes and remains aware of herself, and enjoys the fruits of her labor. We do not know and, most likely, she herself does not know her plans for the future. But it seems logical to assume that one species would not have forged so far ahead of the rest, developing its unique kind of self-aware intelligence, if it had not been evolutionarily important in the destiny of the whole.

The idea of Gaia, in one form or another, has been around for centuries. The North American Indians, as well as other primitive societies in all corners of the world, have long related holistically to their environments, emphasizing the nonlinear, intuitive, and receptive qualities of their Yin natures.

The relatedness with their Earth Mother embraced by those early tribes contained all the elements of religion and mysticism, but lacked the systematic theological structure of the more formal beliefs belonging to religions which became dominant in most of the "civilized" countries.

For those early people whose lives were intimately involved in the natural, experience merged into a common reverence for life. Like the advocates of Gaia, they thought of life as containing all things equally. Living or nonliving, all were joined in one harmoniously cooperative reality. To North American Indians, the white man's insistence on the separation of the one great nature into multiple divisions of mineral, vegetable, and animal—animate and inanimate—with the implied superiority of himself over all made no sense at all. Indians envisioned every object in their experience as being one of the "peoples," all equally imbued with life—some revealed and others not. According to their view, even a stone was an animate being, to be reasonably granted the possibility of speech on appropriate occasions. They felt that those things which had preceded themselves in the order of creation deserved higher status than they, an attitude still reflected in the Indians' profound respect for their elders.

The Indians had no difficulty in accepting the unity between vastly different entities in their environment, relating them all under a common principle. For example, they saw the spider, the bull elk, and the cottonwood tree as united through special relationships with the wind.

Newly hatched spiders began their adventures into the world at the end of a long strand of spun silk cast off to the wind. The whistling call of the mating bull elk was the result of manipulating his breathing instruments in conjunction with the wind. The cottonwood tree, in season, wrapped its seeds in "cotton," and then dispatched each one to its new destiny on the passing wind. Indians saw them all as interconnected, all equal parts of the one inseparable Being, joined through the common element of wind.

Such an intimate feeling between humans and their surroundings formed the basis for every religion at its beginning. The first feeling of reverence stirred in direct response to the natural world, around which all life revolved and depended. Only with time and developing human ego did those feelings fade, leaving a false and inflated sense of humanity's importance in relation to the rest.

A rare opportunity was missed in those early days of our country when the European and Indian cultures came together for the first time, each one containing that which might have added a new dimension to the other. But instead of respecting their differences and exploring the possibilities of a rewarding exchange, they engaged in blind and bitter conflict, dividing the two cultures into oppressed and oppressor, thus increasing the survival vulnerability of them both.

Europeans were quick to label the natives in this strange new land "savages," rating them so far below themselves on their value scale that they felt perfectly justified in enslaving or eliminating as many as they were able, believing these natives to be mere subhuman obstructions standing in the way of their own high purposes.

Had the Indians been an organized power instead of a divided population of scattered tribes, the confrontation might have resulted in a more equitable compromise, with possible far-reaching benefits to both. The Europeans must have seemed an awesome, indomitable force to those people of the simple life who were probably stunned into submission as much as overpowered by such an unfamiliar display of flashy trappings. A bark canoe could not have inspired much confidence next to a flag-flying galleon, nor could the bow and arrow have generated much respect against a booming cannon. The simple needs and beliefs of the Indians were a poor match for the ambition and drive of a more complex, organized, and egotistical invader.

We have almost no working models left of those who practiced coexistence with nature as a living art. Most of the Indian tribes have been scattered, destroyed, or crowded into out-of-the-way reservations, remote corners of barren land that least satisfied the needs and ambitions of their dominant neighbors. Indian children are being lured away from the traditional ways by a fast-moving society that paces itself according to the nervous ticks of the clock. What is left of the tribes has little more than memories to offer its young. A few of the old customs remain, but with a steady drainoff of their original meaning and purpose, as they gradually give way to influences from the outside. There seems no path left for a new Indian generation to follow except for the one of the white man, leading "out there" and away from their own proud heritage.

Ironically, in recent years young white people by the hordes have been turning back to reexamine the simple old beliefs of the native Americans, hoping to rediscover the feeling of connectedness which their own profound sense of alienation tells them they have lost.

I was privileged to enjoy the hospitality of a pueblo in New Mexico at a daylong celebration of dancing and feast, not too many Christmases ago. Though many Indians today are Christian, Christianity has little historical significance in the Indian's religious life. Still a holiday is a holiday, and always a welcomed occasion to stir up the old blood in a rousing reenactment of some of their ancestors' sacred ceremonies.

It was a raw, sunless day with a colorless sky that intermittently scattered stray snowflakes on the flat desert landscape. A few nondescript, forlorn-looking dogs nosed under our elbows to steal a little warmth as we sat huddled on the frozen red clay bank to watch.

The stamp of fringed and moccasined feet, the monotonous, hollow beat of the drums, and the mournful chant of the elders made it easy to fall under the spell. It was also easy to see that at least a shadow of what once had been was still there, even so long after these dances had evolved as an important part of a thriving culture. What the performers had in mind was clearly a great deal more than a dance. What we were seeing was a celebration of nature, a sincere and reverent exercise in praise. Every dancer totally submerged himself in the spirit of the animal he was costumed to represent. He *became* the buffalo, the elk, or the deer. Even though, at the time the dances had been conceived, the man/animal relationship had been that of hunter and hunted, there was nothing of aggression or violence in this expression of it, only profound admiration and respect for the beauty and strength of the animal.

Just one false note was struck in the otherwise moving and authentic re-creation of a time long past. It was not the fault of the Indians, but of the culture which had surrounded and all but overwhelmed them, leaving them stripped of their independence and much of their pride and dignity. The Christmas spirit of the commercial West had seeped past the hallowed bounds of that traditionally nonmaterialistic band of survivors. In one of the intervals between dances, the silent crowd parted to allow passage for one old tribal grandmother who came bearing a basket of gifts for the little boy performers all costumed as deer with their headpieces sprouting real deer's antlers. The old lady wore the usual brightly colored, handwoven blanket draped over her head and shoulders. Her brown, wrinkled face could have been neatly superimposed over the noble profile stamped on many an old U.S nickel (counter to the all-but-extinct buffalo). But the basket that this venerable old native carried was not the handcrafted, sweetgrass masterpiece we might have expected to see, but a dazzling, daffodil-yellow plastic laundry basket, courtesy of the local hardware.

As we outsiders caught our collective breaths, she took the gifts from the basket and, with stoic deliberation, hung them on the prongs of the little boys' antlers. The gifts? Potato chips, Fritos, and salted peanuts, all sanitarily sealed in plastic bags!

A bleak picture, not only for the Indians, but for those of us who have imposed our system even onto those precious few who have clung so long and tenaciously to the very things the rest of us find ourselves so dangerously lacking now. A bleak picture, indeed, if it were not for some of the brighter signs that first lit the horizon some years ago, and still persist as the strongest hope of many.

Above the ominous rumblings of belligerence and greed, and the clash of egos in tooth-and-claw struggles, there is a faint but steady clamor of new voices sounding out from the rest, using invented or resurrected words to communicate their passionate views—words like "ecology," "integration," and "solar"—even new and urgent emphasis on that oft-beleaguered, misinterpreted, misused old standby that has been around forever—"love"!

Most of these voices are emerging from the vast multitudes that made up the "baby boomers" of the fifties and shortly thereafter, grown from the tidal wave of new infants that swamped the maternity wards just after the Korean War, setting the country scrambling to meet the enormous needs of its surprising new bumper crop. They are the ones who, as children, were responsible for that ugly bulge unbalancing population charts of their time that, even yet, persists in their favor. Those were the adolescents who revolutionized the styles of music, the same who flooded the galleries with a profusion of art so different and new that hardly anyone but themselves could understand or appreciate it. They became the far-reaching and the restless, experimenting with mind expansion and alternative lifestyles, looking at themselves and others in shocking (to some) new ways. Some of the most enterprising took to computers like ducks to water. A fair number traveled on shoestrings, gathering degrees like strawberries from universities around the world.

Others stayed to poke their curious noses into every aspect of what the rest of us had been doing, unchallenged, for all of our lives—and they minced no words in passing frank judgment. Some of those audacious youngsters turned their fresh, all-seeing eyes on our sharply divided cities and communities—divided by race, religion, health, wealth, age, and sex. In the light of their youthful idealism, they were shocked and shaken by what they saw. They said so plainly and directly. Then to reinforce their words, they picketed, sat in, chanted, sang, and refused to be silent.

They are older now, and not as volatile as they once were. Some have slipped back into the ways of their parents, lured by the false glitter of short-term interests. But the voices of a lot of them still persist loud and clear, from whatever corner of the country they have scattered. They are up front in all the nuclear, ecological, women's and human rights issues. "It's a nice world," they are saying. "Let's keep it. Bigger is not necessarily better. Small can be beautiful too."

They, along with some of the rest of us, are insisting, with the kind of logic that makes one wonder why someone had not noticed all those things long ago, that it is all right to be black or brown or yellow—or whatever. It is all right to be a woman. It is all right to be single or married—or neither. It is all right to be old, or handicapped, or whatever one naturally is. We are even hearing that it is just as right to be me as it is to be you. "Everyone deserves the same treatment," they are saying. "The world belongs to all of us, not just to those who can afford to buy it."

All this is a stunning turnaround for those who had based their security on Western supremacy, on their color, their sex, their religion, or their bank account, and were confident that any way was the right way as long as it led to bigger and more.

Venturing into uncharted territory is always a risky business. Some of the most promising have become casualties of their own movements. Some have tried to go too far too fast. Some have been misguided, others weak. A few have jumped on the bandwagon without bothering to find out whether that wagon was the right one for them, or in what direction it was heading.

But the sheer number of those who began as a new army of innovative crusaders insures that some of them will prevail, be heard, and have an effect. They have, at least, shaken out the old rug of complacency, revealing to public shame and conscience all those things which had been swept under it for centuries past.

It is from that same mass of youngsters who stormed through crowded classrooms into turbulent adolescence, and on to adulthood, upsetting old standards as they went, and leaving a wake of unprecedented change behind them, that the new heads of management are now emerging. They are crowding into the inner chambers of high-level power. Ideas and impressions go with them. Among them are increasing numbers of women. Differences are already being felt. More will follow just as soon as the power load shifts definitively from the "old guard" to the new.

But the race is still far from won—the race against time and public apathy. Never has so much change been required from so many. How many will respond, and how soon? Nor is it certain that the complex and unwieldy structure of our technological making can be turned to another direction as quickly and decisively as the need seems to be. Whether we still control it, or it now controls us. If we wait too long the course may be irretrievably set—and no one can even be sure that we have not already procrastinated too long.

5
Hear the Music—See the Dance

Scientists with a lyrical turn of mind tell us that every form has its own characteristic "music," and that each object in the room is humming a different tune, outside the range of anyone's hearing, but humming just the same. It is said that cathedrals, with their exquisite proportions, are basically edifices of frozen music. Every object, every statue, every person has its own unique song to sing, depending on its shape and the materials of which it is made. Even you and I, if only we had the ears attuned to hear, are resonating with a strange music, trademark of our own individual selves. The universe, it has been eloquently stated, is essentially a vast system of music.

If, by some magic, we were suddenly to become aware of the normally inaudible sounds surrounding us, it would not only be an incredible, but a hopelessly confusing experience. It is far easier to focus the eye than it is the ear. In a roomful of people it is easy enough to absorb the attention on one face and forget the rest. But, though it is possible to concentrate the listening ear on just one conversation among many, it is virtually impossible to shut out all awareness of others going on at the same time. Nonetheless, such a confusion of conversation would seem as nothing at all compared to suddenly hearing all that was going on in a roomful of knick-knacks humming away at the tops of their atoms!

The inaudible sound coming from any object is extremely small in intensity, issuing from the motion of its atoms and molecules. Molecules are kept in continual activity by whatever heat is contained in the object itself. Everything contains some heat, including objects that may seem very cold to us. Even the molecules in a block of ice are in constant thermal motion. Heat is always relative to whatever we choose to compare it. Thirty-two degrees F seems a reasonably warm winter's day in New England. Yet, the same temperature, were it to occur in Florida at the same time of year, would be considered decidedly cooler.

It is easy to imagine that a piece of metal might be chilled to a temperature low enough to stop all thermal motion of its molecules. In theory, this ultimate freeze is referred to as absolute zero and, conceivably, nothing could be any colder than that. In actuality, however, it is believed that such a state could never really be achieved, since there could never be anything totally devoid of heat and, therefore, without some motion of its molecules.

We might compare sound, heard or unheard, with heat. In a particularly fanciful mood, one could even envision all objects, and even our own selves, as alive with dancing atoms and molecules, which at the same time are broadcasting unique patterns of tones—music—according to the shape and content of its source. A living being necessarily emits a more complicated set of sound patterns than an inanimate object, due to the chemical reactions going on inside its body, as well as the interaction of atoms with each other and even the patterns of waves inside the atoms. Clearly, the hum that we are humming is more on the order of a symphony of infinite variety than it is a simple ditty.

Seeing the universe in terms of music and dance is a refreshing change from the old Newtonian concept of matter consisting of clusters of "billiard balls" that behaved strictly according to the principles of cause and effect. It must have been a great surprise to a lot of somber intellectuals to catch those fey little leprechauns of the laboratories in their true musical colors. The description of an atom leaves hardly anything to hang a thought on—the atom being mainly empty space and rhythmic movement. The ultimate reason for an atom has to do with its dynamic form, and the dynamic aspect consists of vibration with harmonic relations. (That does sound a long way from billiard balls, and a lot like music!)

Expanding our vision to the unimaginable scope of the universe, we can see that the sweeping movements of the gigantic galaxies are just as faithful to their own particular rhythms as are the atoms of a smallness equally incomprehensible. So precisely timed are the cyclic rhythms of those great cosmic communities and the bodies within them that the path of one hardly ever interferes with that of another. Astronomers on Earth are able to make precise predictions of celestial events long before they occur, and even trace back through light years in time to events that took place long before there was anyone around to record them.

Within the larger rhythms of the galaxies, individual suns and planets with spins, rhythms, and oscillations of their own are each adding other notes to the complex harmony of the whole. Our own sun is seen by astronomers as a fairly ho-hum, middle-sized star, representative of countless others within the range of their telescopes. Yet closer examination discloses the familiar golden and glowing orb to be ringing away, oscillating regularly in precise patterns of frequencies and spatial scales with a clear, bell-like resonance. At the same time, solar winds are creating an interplanetary magnetic field, and pulling part of the sun's coronal magnetic field into interplanetary space in a giant configuration resembling a pinwheel. To us here on Earth, it would appear to be rotating about once every twenty-seven days.

Considering the inevitable effects of all those cycles showing up in our time, tides, seasons, and weather, it is no wonder that our bodies, being made up of energy patterns themselves, respond in regular physical and behavior cycles of their own. Cycles of energy, cycles of appetite and sleep, as well as a great many others are choreographed by nature to keep us in harmony with that which is going on all around and within us.

Every living thing on planet Earth has its own inner clocks set to keep its natural cycles ticking away in tune with the rest. Take the fiddler crab. His color is darker during the day and fades to a lighter color with the coming of night. At low tide he scurries about enjoying peak energy, only to retreat to some safe haven as the tide rises. Transport this little fellow far away to the desert, and he will still respond on schedule to the same rhythms, precisely as they had been set for him in the beginning.

We humans rooted, as we are, in a ground of waves and forces, influence and respond to the ones that surround and bombard us from every side. Some, which fall within the very narrow range of perception by our physical senses, are recognized as music, human speech, color, light, or something else. But there are untold others of which we are consciously unaware. Who knows from how far away in space or time such influences come—or how far past our own personal boundaries those we are sending may travel.

Individuals appear into existence as suddenly as a bubble in a boiling pot of water, and remain for hardly the flick of a cosmic eye. They erupt into an interconnected network of fields and patterns, necessitating a new arrangement in the vicinity of their becoming. Surrounding waves and forces influence their adjustment in small, or not so small, ways. Then, like the bubble, when any particular pattern has spent its time and is unable to hold its own against cancellation by other stronger forces, it blends into the larger order, dispersed to become part of the whole once more—like cards returned to the deck, ready for a new hand.

Existence, as it turns out, has to do with regularity and order. It is the chaos of something gone wrong, "out of tune" rhythms, that paves the way for potential disaster. A well functioning living system is an integrated structure, a harmonic arrangement of vibrations in mathematically precise patterns that resemble the highest orders of music, dance, or any of the other great arts.

Among the countless harmonic patterns making up living beings, variety is achieved by unique arrangements of a surprisingly spare set of the same essential ingredients. Through slight variations on the same theme, nature has managed to be impressively creative with a very small bag of tricks.

All living things share the common denominator of just four types of simple molecules called "nucleotides." These molecules are strung together like beads on a chain. They come in double strands knit into a symmetry of atoms that make up the twisted molecule known as DNA. This tiny marvel is packed with all the information the potential being will need for a lifetime of development—information that will be available at exactly the right time, under appropriate conditions. Like musical notes on tape, only subtle differences in the arrangement of DNA's four factors instruct whether the tune to be played will be man, mouse, mosquito, or monkey.

Though the double helix DNA is the key pattern, and remains unchanged throughout the lifetime of the individual, still the collection of atoms and molecules within the helix is continuously in the process of replacement. It would seem that only the ghostly pattern of one's self survives to the end, and the material reality is just the expendable means of ensuring the existence of individual expression in its own terms on Earth.

Long before the harmonious rhythms of nature could be understood rationally, they had found a place of meaning in the old myths and religions, and were acted out in rituals and religious practices. In addition, humanity was quick to invent new ways of creating others directed toward some practical or pleasurable end. How long ago did we learn that a gentle lullaby would soothe a restless child, or that the steady, hypnotic beat of a drum would excite emotions to the pitch necessary for risking one's life in battle? The hard-rock beat of popular music still rouses mass frenzy. The right tempo and the right pitch have long been employed to open the mind to trance states. Old medicine men, adepts, mystics, and warriors were all familiar with the mysterious power of rhythm in influencing the human brain. Now modern psychologists and neuroscientists are taking another look. Mind-brain technology has become one of the hottest of their issues. If, as they believe, any of the full range of human emotions can be stimulated to a high degree with the appropriate wave form and frequency, a whole new hornet's nest of sticky decisions may crop up to be made by the leaders of tomorrow.

Nearly everyone learns his first lesson of "going with the waves" on the playground swing. If a child is given a gentle push each time he reaches the rope's limit, at the precise moment of its readiness to return, the speed and endurance of his airy flight are pronounced and prolonged. He is being helped along in the way things want to go naturally. The "pusher" and the "pushed" are in tune, participants in a harmony of motion.

If, however, the child is pushed before the swing has reached its critical point of return, the push is met with instant and stubborn resistance, canceling most of its energy, and interfering with its smoothness in a confused and chaotic tangle of waves. The force of the push is out of tune with the natural wave of the swing's sweep. The surfer, to avoid a wipeout, needs to practice the "feel" of the wave he is trying to catch, and to train himself to submit to its rhythm, avoiding any counter motions by himself.

There are waves of fashion, speech, behavior, music, and a whole lot more. A few well timed pushes by enough people in the direction the wave is naturally inclining greatly enhances its strength and ability to survive. Contributing "pushers" are likely to feel comfortably "in tune" with their own time and its action, as well.

To change the direction of an existing wave requires creating another of sufficient strength to counteract and finally cancel the old—with a strong, natural momentum of its own. It takes time, as well as creation of a frustrating and disorderly interim of interfering waves, both locked in an all out struggle for survival. To achieve success, the new wave must be stronger, more persistent, and better timed than the old.

Great changes in history usually occur after long periods of suffering and strife in a duel of opposing forces. One force eventually prevails in overcoming the effectiveness of the other, thereby allowing itself free movement ahead. Harmony is restored for a time, helped along or weakened by other smaller waves that intervene but do not have the strength to dominate. However, in all likelihood the prevailing wave will sooner or later be challenged by another with formidable canceling power, and once again the turn of events will hang in balance.

Although we may not be consciously aware of the fundamental rhythms, we sometimes sense their presence through mood changes that regularly affect our behavior—the ups and downs we all feel to be outside our control. There are those days, or even extended periods, when we feel "in tune" with no conscious effort of our own, those heady times when good fortune seems to rain on our unsuspecting heads, the times of giant steps ahead, individual strengths heightened, and choices satisfyingly affirmed. Times like those are commonly and loosely described as "luck" or even a "gift from God," and attract superstitions like flies around a honey pot.

Unfortunately, the possibility of anyone depending too much on such ill-founded confidence is usually modified by those equally mysterious, counterbalancing days, periods or events when "bad luck" or "ill fortune" seems to cast dark shadows on even the best directed and most diligent efforts—when unsuspected obstacles arise at every turn, and even normal endeavors turn out disaster-prone. In some out-of-the-way pockets of Earth, responsibility for that kind of "luck" is often attributed to evil spirits, curses, or some other kind of witchcraft. Anyone in the throes of such a "spell" is susceptible to believing much the same thing, whatever one's cultural background.

Then, apart from the more common regular shifting from gain to loss and back again, there is that single incident which crops up in a sea of ordinary ones, defying any category of explanation, appearing like a lightning bolt from a clear sky. A slipping together of just the right circumstances occurs when, in one electrifying instant, underlying connections of which we have been unaware come together with startling ease and grace. C. G. Jung called such slipping together *synchronicity,* and this is what he had to say about it:

> Synchronicity is not a philosophical view but an empirical concept which postulates an intellectually necessary principle. This cannot be called either materialism or metaphysics. . . . Synchronicity is no more baffling or mysterious than the discontinuities of physics. It is

> only the ingrained belief in the sovereign power of causality that creates intellectual difficulties and makes it appear unthinkable that causeless events exist or could ever occur. But if they do, then we must regard them as creative acts, as the continuous creation of a pattern that exists from all eternity, repeats itself sporadically, and is not derivable from any known antecedents. . . . Meaningful coincidences are thinkable as pure chance. But the more they multiply and the greater and more exact the correspondence is, the more their probability sinks and their unthinkability increases, until they can no longer be regarded as pure chance but, for a lack of causal explanation, have to be thought of as meaningful arrangements.

Pure chance or ''meaningful arrangement''? Most synchronicities happen frequently in small ways, startling enough for the moment, but soon forgotten. We are thinking of a friend. The telephone rings—it is that friend. But that once-in-a-lifetime, dramatic coming together of seemingly unrelated parts that adds up to a perfect whole is an experience that sticks in the reasonable mind like a bone in the throat.

One of those sudden jolts of logic happened to me in my semi-starving art school days in a city far from home. The shoestring on which I was seeing my way through school had come to an abrupt end some time before the summer classes I was attending were scheduled to conclude. Fortunately, my shrinking resources had begun to take a serious turn at about the same time the local markets were overflowing with a bumper crop of green grapes. Those were the days of hamburgers for a nickel and all the grapes one could eat for a quarter, so bodily survival was easy enough, however limited the menu. Still, the pattern of my creeping poverty continued to unfold, until the hard fact of reality was there to be faced—the monthly rent was due, and I lacked the funds to pay it.

I lived in a rooming house with a lot of other, equally strapped students. Our landlady of the calcified heart had a survival policy that was direct and to the point—no rent, no room. Her record was unscathed. She had never been known to grant a reprieve.

As far as I could see, every possible resource had gone bone dry. There was absolutely no route through which sudden riches might flow. But, in spite of the apparent hopelessness of my dilemma, I managed to maintain surprisingly good (and unreasonable) spirits. "Something will turn up," I promised myself, right up to and including the final day of reckoning.

On the afternoon of The Day, I sat down to ponder a bleak future. I had been unable to come up with any lawful alternative to spending the oncoming days—weeks? months? years? (possibly forever)—as a homeless bag lady, unless of course I were to abandon cherished career plans and retreat home which, at that time, seemed even worse.

I was roused from my reveries by a knock on the door. I suspected it might be the landlady with extended palm. It was a girl I knew only slightly, carrying her suitcase. She had once lived in a room near mine, and had moved to another part of the city some time before. I had not seen her since. She seemed bursting with good cheer. "If I can stay with you for a couple of weeks," she began, "I will pay the rent and help with the food."

It turned out that she was soon to be married. A good Catholic, she hoped to find a place to stay in her old neighborhood while she made plans for the wedding in her favorite parish, officiated over by her favorite priest. "I thought of you," she said, "and I wondered if you wouldn't mind. . .?" (Wouldn't *mind*?!) Within the two weeks, I found myself a temporary job to tide me safely over until term's end.

At the time, I was riding the natural waves with the confidence of an old surfing pro. I loved where I was and what I was doing. I was fulfilling my dearest ambition, and one for which I felt myself to be a "natural." My attitude was positive in every way. It seems not unlikely that, when my efforts fell short, the needed ingredient slipped into the void to keep the positive momentum flowing. The pattern was set. It was like the missing arm of a starfish—the pattern reconstructs that which is needed to complete the whole. Or like a holographic pattern, in which the whole is present in each of the parts.

6
Between Me and Thee

Among practitioners of the arts, the poets' task may be hardest of them all. They are the instruments through which abstract principles of being, inherent in their knowing but transcending form or words, grope for approximation through form and words. Harmony and emotional patterns that poets feel are spontaneous and boundless, but their only means of expressing them must be the linear word-form of time language—a bottleneck if ever there was one.

But poets face their challenging task bravely, and often do remarkably well by it, driven as they are by the irrepressible human urge to communicate. They rely for interpretation of their efforts on the same archetypal principles being equally inherent in the mind of the receiver. They know their function to be setting off the spark to activate an echo.

Lu Chi, a Chinese poet, pondered the challenge with these words:

> We poets struggle with Non-being to force it to yield being.
> We knock upon silence for an answering music.

Acknowledge the Wonder

We enclose boundless space in a square foot of paper.
We pour out deluge from the inch space of the heart.

Humans, as far as we know, are the only ones who have broken through the barrier between inner and outer, expressing what they think and feel through spoken and written language.

Language comes to human infants naturally and easily, as much a part of the plan of them as the sprouting of their teeth. They come into the world predisposed and ready for language. From their very first breath, they are indoctrinated into the tongue of their parents. Even before they have had time to discover their ability to think, they are being supplied with what its basic structure is to be. They begin almost immediately to respond with pleasure to sound patterns that conform to their own deep structure of language. Only the surface details need to be added. They not so much "learn" as "catch" the sense of it, once exposed.

Just as soon as they grasp the notion of language, they are able to be charmingly creative in its use. No parrots, they, simply repeating words and sentences they have heard. They come equipped with an implicit if, as yet, unformed generative grammar in their own special DNA information system. As soon as development and conditions allow, they strive to make it explicit and individual.

In addition, those brand new little humans have at their disposal, for whatever uniquely personal use they choose to make of it, the accumulated information of all communicating ancestors who came and went before them. It is on their shoulders that the child is invited to stand. It seems that the quantity and quality of the space-age newborn's brain is actually no different from that of the long-ago Stone Age infant's. The difference between what he will become, compared to the little chap chewing on bones in the family cave, is due solely to the vast store of cultural information awaiting the latecomer. Nothing more than his so-recent happening in the long chain of human learning and discovery allows him the opportunity to some day explore outer space rather than hunt mammoths with a stone axe.

The evolutionary gift of universal language that comes with every human child is genetically programmed to accommodate languages falling within a narrow band of possibilities. All people on the planet Earth, presumably evolving from a single or similar source, create their languages from within that narrow band of possibilities. Children do not have too much difficulty learning the language of their parents, since all subscribe to the same inborn, universal grammar.

The difficulty for some children of some languages will come later when they must attempt to apply the linear, logical thought of their culture to the nonlinear, often illogical dimension that surrounds them. Every language is built around the dominant or prevailing view of reality of that particular culture. The view tends to project into the language. To express a personal view contrary to the prevailing one is extremely difficult, if not impossible, if one uses the standard form in the regular way.

The English language, with its subject-verb-object structure, reflects a view of fragmentation, separation, and parts. That view is deeply embedded in our thinking, and operative at every level of our society. It is a product of the old Newtonian physics, pictured as a grid with all points entirely outside of each other, and only contiguous relation among them. It is a world view founded on a set of basic particles of a fixed nature.

The discoveries of modern quantum physics, the ''enfolded order'' of physicist David Bohm, and the holographic theories of neuroscientist Karl Pribram present quite a different view. Their reality emerges as an inseparable, interconnected, and continuing event, of which ''things'' are seen only as appearances abstracted from the whole. Language appropriate to that kind of reality would necessarily place greater emphasis on its verbs than on its nouns. As the late Buckminster Fuller once mused, ''I seem to be a verb.''

Poetry, at its best, is a better indicator of such a process of existence than is most prose. In music and dance, parts merge into an interconnected whole in the natural way. Film and animation are easy communicators of a nonstationary reality. But, clearly, doing justice to the notion of a simultaneous, multifaceted, single whole, in place of the old limited, linear view of fixed form and separate existence, will challenge the best efforts of parents, teachers, and creative artists for generations to come.

Language, with its content as food for the growing mind, is the most direct route to a child's understanding, and so bears an important share of the responsibility for creating wise and sensible methods of dealing with the unprecedented human problems that are now building to confront generations of the future.

At least in part, the structure of human language reflects the structure of the human brain. Language, through symbol, has evolved to handle the specifics of left brain, Yang reasoning, and at the same time has remained flexible enough to allow expression of the more spontaneous, abstract, Yin impulses of myth, poetry, and religion originating in the right brain area.

In the natural order of things, systems of all kinds develop from simplicity toward greater and greater complexity. It could be expected that the brain and its language would follow the same basic plan. In its present state, the wrinkled little cauliflower-like human brain is something of a "triune" organ, having undergone dramatic changes since accommodating its reptile forebears, then on to the lower mammals, and eventually to the human creature. Time saw fit, for reasons of its own, to preserve the outgrown brain sections rather than to discard them. Each new addition was simply folded over the old, resulting in one brain in which all past developmental areas coexist with the very latest. The most recent addition, which makes up the cerebrum or forebrain, is responsible for the complexity of today's human intelligence. However, the reptilian and paleomammalian behaviors still lurk ominously, buried deep in the dark recesses of the contemporary human's high-browed cranium.

There is no reason to believe that the on-going development of the brain and its functioning intelligence has peaked in our time. More likely, it is still moving ahead on schedule, according to its own leisurely (or not so leisurely) pace. The center of a process is not the best place from which to evaluate it.

Finely tuned and trained intelligence through technology accounts for the comparatively sudden tidal wave of knowledge and understanding that has all but engulfed our minds, and begun to change the way we think. Electronics, a spinoff of quantum mechanics, produced the computer. It is believed that optical fibers, by which information is communicated on waves of light, will be the technology of tomorrow, reducing the bulk even further, and enormously increasing the amount of information potentially transmittable.

It is easy to see that, within the last century, intelligence and its operation have taken an unprecedented outward turn. It may simply be that there is no longer any room to add yet another advanced section to the already existing biological brain. The protective, boney shell encasing it appears to be packed to capacity. Enlarging the structure of the infant's skull would be no solution, since it must conform to the size of the mother's pelvis, if passage for the child is to be allowed. Due to gravitational influences, no living being can grow beyond a certain point and still function at maximum efficiency in its intended capacity. And, since the size of the skeletal framework of our kind has remained within about the same range for thousands of years, it seems likely that the humanoid has reached its practical outer size limit. Without dramatic changes in the basic structure, the size of the brain probably must remain at about what it is now.

It is still too early to view the effects of the computer revolution with the objectivity of distance. But there is no mistaking that it has extended the brain's capacity far beyond its previous normal range. Any brain can process and communicate information more rapidly, efficiently, and accurately in tandem with a computer than it can by itself. Nature, immune from the human hangup of distinctions between "inner" and "outer," in its adaptive ingenuity is reaching beyond the biological form to add the next degree of intellectual complexity to meet the needs of a new and more complex age.

Early social prophets predicted a smothering conformity to follow in the wake of the computer. In actuality, quite the opposite appears to be occurring. Those electronic aids are able to offer individuals a multitude of alternatives, allowing them to personalize their choices with a precision and refinement far beyond their natural capabilities. Due to the elimination of tedious physical effort and time-consuming steps of mental logic, the individual has access to an immeasurably enlarged field of operation. Consolidated information that can be put on hold (stored), without bulk or memory loss, is producing an ever-growing bank of riches for anyone to draw upon—a kind of omniscient body of human understanding and ingenuity in the making.

Through all those vastly improved methods of communication, individual units of human intelligence are gaining the strength of unity. It would, however, be unwise and premature to assume that this small Earth-planet bears the monopoly of a reasoning and communicating intelligence. There are an estimated one hundred billion galaxies and, at least, an equal number of stars in each one. That a few of those stars in the order of our sun must have orbiting planets is a reasonable assumption. Even more convincingly, scientists claim a tendency of galactic clouds (building blocks of everything) to form organic or carbon-based compounds rather than inorganic structures of silicon or metals. Those organic compounds are the basic ingredients of all that will eventually evolve into life. Thus, it seems safe to speculate that life must thrive in countless other forms and places apart from the human and this planet.

We have barely ventured beyond the limits of our own modest Earth to experience some of the mystery that has intrigued us since our first wondering awareness of the sky. Magnificent as the space probes may appear to the Earthbound, none has yet more than dipped a tentative toe into the marvels that must surely lie beyond anyone's wildest fantasies. Away from their own environment, earthlings are incredibly frail and vulnerable little beings, totally dependent on the small bits of earth they must bring with them to survive. They are still firmly attached to Mother Earth's apron strings, and it is unlikely she will ever let them go completely.

Considering our innate curiosity and our ingenious methods of satisfying it, it is almost inevitable that sooner or later we will be confronted by someone or something who (or that) will challenge our lofty, self-imposed image of superiority. What this being has to say, and the means by which he or she chooses to say it, will mark a crucial point in human history—for better or worse and forever after. One can only hope that the meeting, when and if it occurs, will be delayed until we Earth-humans have had time to mature a little more. Our relations with our near neighbors have not been exemplary. Any species other than our own (and even a considerable number of our own) have been mostly regarded in terms of their usefulness. Unless the egotistical notion of ourselves in relation to others of a different kind undergoes a cleansing enlightenment in the meantime, our attitude toward any outside contacts would probably be the same.

We humans have always been inclined to press our noses to a mirror and believe we were looking from a window onto the cosmos. We are suspicious of strangers with a difference. Our suspicions include not only the E. T.'s that, so far, exist only in imagination, but those who inhabit the very same planet and see it through the eyes of another species, or even race.

It should be no surprise that, with our newly aroused interest in animal behavior, the greatest delight comes in discovering animal qualities that are weak reflections of our own. Through a few dedicated human trainers turned foster parents, a handful of scientists, and a curious public to encourage them, attempts are being made to decipher the "language" of some animals (in human terms of course), and even to strike up some kind of a rapport with them. As one would expect, research with our close cousins, the great apes, attracts the greatest public interest and attention.

Most animals hold firmly to the boundaries of their own kind, showing little interest in becoming more "human," and unimpressed by the great opportunity being offered to up-grade their communication system to ours. A few, carefully trained over long periods of time, have learned some simple words and sentences, using human sign language for the deaf. However, none has shown the slightest inclination to divulge any strictly ape-like secrets of being, or shown much interest in our kind of intellectuality. Any human child of two, given only half the time and effort spent on those animals, would be a comparative genius with his or her linguistic skill and creativity.

The animal brain is not programmed for language or speech. Trained animals interested in pleasing their trainers (who usually give them rewards of food) are struggling against their own natural communication programming. The "grammar" appropriate to their animal needs, and having served them well for thousands of years, is simply set to follow different rules. No doubt, we would have just as difficult a time in getting the hang of their pattern of thinking as they do with ours.

Words as symbols are not necessarily the key to all other communication systems. It is believed that dolphins, with their oversized brains and wide range of clicks and whistles, communicate in "acoustic pictures." John C. Lilly, scientist, author, and pioneer in altered states, has spent a great deal of time studying the behavior of dolphins. He is attempting to create a dolphin computer language based on sonic codes. Such a system, besides sifting out the messages from the noise of dolphins (much of which is beyond the range of the human ear) and the songs of the humpback whale, might prove useful in determining whether the noises our listening radio telescopes are hearing is concealing any intelligent overtures from the great beyond.

It seems ironic that human interest in animals, as creatures in their own right, was largely nonexistent until most of them were balanced precariously on the edge of extinction. For centuries, wild animals were regarded as having no rights of their own, their only purpose to provide food or sport for the hunter. Beyond contributing to human needs, they were expected to stay out of the way, and amicably retreat as man advanced on their territory. Now, too late for a lot of them, they seem to have nudged their way to a reckoning in the human economy. Television program planners love them. Animal documentaries cover a broad span of potential viewers of all ages, all interests. Expensive safaris have become the "in" thing for vacationers who travel the world over to "oh" and "ah" at the few lonely survivors of a once rich, wild ecosystem.

Animals that have been living in close proximity to humans for untold centuries have fared somewhat better, due mainly to their adaptability to other ways and their patient and uncritical acceptance of life as they find it. Startling examples crop up regularly that show how much better some species are at entering our world and acting intelligently in it than we ever would be in theirs.

I once shared several years of my life with a small brown and bright-eyed dachshund I called Hartley. (What she called *me* in private communication with friends of her own kind, I was never privileged to know.) Though each of us reserved specific periods of the day for ourselves, periods totally devoid of interest to the other, we did have some things in common that we both regarded with uncommon passion.

The beach was one. Odd couple though we were, our responses proved identical when confronted with a long stretch of warm sand edged with blue, lacy, lapping water. In each of us the uncontrollable urge was invariably roused to loll, stroll, walk, or jog, depending on the height and angle of the sun. Those outings became an all-season, early morning ritual that neither of us would have missed for anything, barring debilitating disaster.

The trouble was that as soon as the water had sunned much beyond the freezing point in this northern edge of New England, I set about changing my routine by donning a bathing suit, beach robe and carrying a beach towel. My intent was to jog, swim, then enjoy the sun, thus tripling enjoyment of the morning's small fraction I had allowed away from my desk. We lived only across the street from the beach. Once over the wall, I dropped the towel and robe on the sand to jog on unencumbered.

It was clear from the beginning that we had a problem, or, to be more precise, that Hartley had a problem. So embedded was her sense of loyalty and need to protect that to leave my belongings unattended—vulnerable to theft, outside takeover, or heaven-only-knew what else—was more than she could comfortably bring herself to consider. In spite of all reassurance and coaxing, Hartley elected to stand guard, muscles taut and trembling, wistfully straining to watch as I jogged on down the water's edge alone. She hardly moved until I had safely returned, ready for a changing of the guard, in charge of my own possessions in my curiously haphazard human way.

For several days, Hartley's sense of duty suffered against her urge to enjoy. Her ears and tail drooped in a pathetic expression of defeat. There seemed just no way that she could attend to her responsibilities and her own pleasure at one and the same time.

Or was there? A few mornings into the frustration, she left the house with a new spring in her steps, a new light in her eye. I dropped my paraphernalia as usual, jogging heartlessly off. I looked back, expecting to see my loyal friend hunched on the terry mound, as usual. Not so at all. This time she was not frozen into guard position, agonizingly enduring her sacrifice for my benefit. What I saw was a small, brown dynamo furiously digging and kicking up the sand, raining it down on the terry heap—higher, higher—until all that remained was an untidy pyramid of sand.

In almost less time than it takes to tell, she was on her way, streaking to catch up, one small tongue-and-tail propelled brown rocket! Every inch of her (and there were proportionately more inches of her than anyone would reasonably expect) was quivering with the kind of joy ordinarily reserved for fresh bones, stray cats, and tennis balls. Her conscience was clear. The treasures were safely buried against marauding intruders. She had figured a way and legitimately earned her freedom.

Each morning from then until the chill winds of autumn, Hartley did the same thing. Needless to say, she quickly became a small celebrity among the few early morning beachers who applauded her "almost human" way of resolving a dog's dilemma.

7
In the Eye of the Beholder

One of my most cherished memories of a visit to New York has to do with reflections. A friend and I watched a production *outside* the Museum of Modern Art that probably equaled or surpassed anything on the inside. Yet, among all the busy, bustling goal-seekers, we were alone in our awareness of that delightful, early morning fantasy going on endlessly, and free for the noticing. The museum was closed, but the reflection of a continuous stream of moving cars and people on a curved glass door—miniaturized and vertically distorted to utterly intriguing, gnome-like images—held us spellbound, longer I suspect than any single work of art displayed in the galleries would have.

Reflection is a kind of shadow, one of the most persistent facts of everyday life, yet largely ignored for its complete lack of utility by almost everyone but children, the simple-minded, and a playful kitten now and then.

There are moving and stationary shadows. None of them is ever the same. Everything influences them—the time of day, season of the year, weather, and climate. But their very being depends on the eye that perceives and the mind that attends them. Shadows can come and go in a flash, coming from nowhere and leaving nothing behind. Though shadows have acquired a gloomy reputation, they frolic in the sun and go into deep mourning when it departs the earth.

One of the most elegant shadow/reflections of all is the silver and gold honeycomb that quivers through clear, shallow water in the light of the sun. When conditions are just right, the shimmering and shifting, expanding and contracting never fall out of basic orderliness. The impression is there for anyone with a ready eye and an alert and registering mind.

Such subtle forms of beauty, common enough to have escaped the notice of so many, cannot be choreographed, rehearsed, stored, or replayed. Immediacy is of their essence. Enjoyment of them is abundantly available to anyone everywhere, as universal and democratic as anything could be. A shadow or reflection shows itself in the same light to everyone. The shadow of a beggar is just as transparent and delicate as the shadow of a king. Hovel or castle reflect equally in puddle or in moat. There is no prejudice or preference. Those are the prerogatives of the observing eye.

An aesthetic sense is a natural characteristic of the human psyche. Watch any infant who has just discovered seeing catch the brightest spot of color within range, and fasten on it with unwavering satisfaction. Already the sense is that someday survival may depend on the ability to distinguish truth from falsehood. Instinctively, an infant recognizes the beautiful to be one's most dependable guide to the truth.

As time passes, natural impulses give way to the child's right of choice. Unfortunately, all too often, the demands of daily living crowd out the more contemplative aspects of an individual's nature. Beauty, if not materially redeemable, drops to the bottom of the value scale. But whether anyone is to experience the world as filled with beauty or something less will depend on that person's unique response to the everyday. If keeping the heart and mind open and a sense of wonder alive and alert can be managed, then beauty is there to be seen everywhere like a pervading translucence, or the mysterious glow from another order. As with the medieval science of alchemy, that individual will have mastered the art of transforming the common into something precious.

On the other hand, if one's adult senses have been allowed to become jaded or dulled, that person may begin a dreary search for artificial stimulation to compensate for those lost satisfactions and pleasures remembered from the open vision of childhood. But such efforts serve poorly to relieve the drab routine of a graceless existence.

Everywhere, natural laws express through a beautifully patterning nature. From the elegant swirl of a galaxy, the pleasing configuration of a flower, a living being, a crystal, or a snowflake, symmetry is a natural and, seemingly, essential element of reality, and accessible to human experience everywhere. In search of dependable guidelines, scientists have discovered that nature's way of revealing its hidden truths is, likewise, one of simplicity and beauty. Einstein's highest seal of approval on one of his equations was describing it as beautiful. His aesthetic sense helped him know when something "looked" right or "felt" wrong. Without ever really understanding why, most of us do the same in our more modest ways.

Probably more than people of any other culture, the Japanese profoundly understand and regularly practice the art of a simple and unadorned beauty. As a result, their most ordinary experiences are transformed by their refined sense of essences, creating a level of everyday living that is probably unequaled anywhere. Their tiny, postage-stamp gardens are deeply satisfying to the receptive eye, as are their homes, food, manners, and dress. (I am thinking of the traditional, and not those habits and styles which, increasingly and regrettably, are being borrowed from the West.)

The tourist who enters Japan expecting nothing more than the gaudy trinkets and novelties to be found on souvenir stands at any public attraction the world over, or even the up-to-date, cleverly innovative TVs, watches, radios, cameras, computers, or automobiles, is due for a shocking surprise. The Japanese are first-rate competitors, and unusually skilled in flooding the markets of the world's four corners with just the kind of product the local people are likely to favor most. But they, themselves, do not necessarily subscribe to such common tastes. The best of what they produce is reserved for their own enjoyment, and underlying those things is a firm and penetrating grasp of just what it is that makes for a mature and refined beauty.

The tea ceremony, flower arranging, sumi painting, and haiku, with their gently unassuming air, may escape the notice of many a hurried traveler, but they are deeply entrenched in the Japanese culture. Few others are able to understand and appreciate them as well. It is almost as though those people were speaking among themselves in a secret language, purposely hidden from all who experience on a coarser level—and to whom they would have little to say anyway.

The Japanese people are small. Their country of islands is small. Most of their houses are tiny, and include only a minimum of garden space, if any at all. But over the centuries they have cleverly woven a veil of illusion, transforming their insufficiencies with simplicity, good taste, and an understanding of basic principles. In the midst of what might have been intolerable crowding, confusion, and chaos, they have created the feeling of space, of peace, and a highly developed sense of privacy for themselves and others.

The Japanese are careful to work with nature, rather than against it. They make no effort to control, only to assist in the direction the natural appears to be inclining anyway. They do not use, but allow themselves to be used by it. The result is a subtle intensification and definition of the best of the natural. Their gardens are masterpieces of noninterference and cooperation. Even their paintings reflect this recognition and acceptance of humanity's place and importance in the context of the whole. Often human figures in their works, instead of dominating all else as they commonly do in the West, are delicately integrated into the rest of the scenery, modestly assuming their natural proportions.

Though Tokyo is one of the most densely populated cities in the world, a visitor is instantly struck by the order and quiet efficiency of its busy streets. On the immaculate, well-run, *on-time* subways and trains (where attendants wear clean white gloves!), and from the crowds of people everywhere, one encounters the kind of capable understatement and mass courtesy that makes for the most extreme case of culture shock in reentering one's own country, or almost any other, afterwards.

To understand the ways of those incredible people is to know something of the development of their primary art—the art of survival, fostered and strengthened throughout their long and turbulent history fraught with fire, flood, earthquake, and war. Their flimsy paper and wood houses are particularly vulnerable to fire. The country on a series of small islands is surrounded by a mighty and unpredictable sea. There are 196 volcanoes of which 30 are active, making for frequent earth tremors and the ever-present fear of a major earthquake. Much of Tokyo was destroyed in the Kanto earthquake of 1923 when more than 110,000 people died. In addition, during the last war, Tokyo was raided 70 times within a year. A great part of it was wiped out again. To make matters even worse, at the war's end, the country staggered under two devastating atomic blasts that resulted in the mutilation and death of thousands, culminating in the country's debilitating and humiliating defeat.

Without strong inner resources, based on long-standing tradition, the Japanese people might have toppled under so much pain and tragedy. Instead, they promptly busied themselves with that which had been left to them, rising to prominence among the world's leading industrial powers in an astonishingly short time—in many instances beating the long time industrialists at their own game.

Those resourceful people have clearly demonstrated the formidable strength of a delicate beauty. By seeing grandeur in their disasters and beauty in their pain, that which threatened to crush the spirit became endurable. The pomp and ceremony that attended their wars helped to soften the horror. Nothing is so dreadful that it cannot be relieved by the mind's quiet contemplation of its inseparable relation to the whole.

There is some common element in beauty and pain. There is an unmistakable aura of sadness haunting the most exquisite beauty. Something almost too lovely to bear brings tears to the eyes. The Japanese are acutely sensitive to this paradox, and their concepts of beauty are filled with an awareness of it. The air of poignant melancholy present in some things—rust on an iron kettle, lichens growing on a rock, blossoms fallen from a tree, or the moon subdued behind a veil of mist—are described by the Japanese as *sabi,* meaning rusty, tarnished, lonely, and *wabi* to indicate a haunting sense of desolation, forlornness, or abandonment. Anyone can identify with those feelings when confronted with a beauty so intense that it seems to overpower. Such feelings have been obliquely described as a homesickness, or the stirring of some long-forgotten, or half-forgotten beauty once known—and that someday may be known again. It could be what beauty is all about, intertwined with truth in some mysterious way, as it seems to be.

Absolute beauty is impossible to perceive in a world based on relativities. There is always something of the Yang in every Yin, a little of the evil in every good, and something always tantalizingly between the eye and the absolute. No true work of art can be anything more than a finger pointing to the moon, indicating, through its symbolic language, the direction in which the moon itself lies. The value of any work depends on its particular strength in stirring latent racial memories in the collective mind of the viewer's subconscious. Such messages are impossible to convey directly. The art must rely on those symbols which have evolved over the centuries by slow accumulation of human experience, like the steady accretion of stalactites in a subterranean cave.

The Japanese are masters of suggestibility in art—the empty spaces, the economy of line and color, inviting the viewer to participate in a search for the inexpressible. Sensitive artists exercise careful restraint to keep from spelling out their inspiration in too great detail. Spaces need to be left for filling in with the feelings and experiences brought by the viewer. There may be some among those viewers who will be able to catch the merest suggestion, and carry it past even the artist's limits. By circumventing any known shape whatsoever, the artist can leave the field open to an ever wider spectrum of interpretation, avoiding involvement with the previous associations and stereotypic reactions of the audience.

The roots of beauty go immeasurably deeper than a mere prettiness. We tire quickly of the shallowness of nothing more than surface glitter. Beauty of the highest order does not offer itself so easily. Something must always be sensed beyond—left unsaid, unborn—inviting the observer to become involved in discovering that elusive, less-than-obvious message that is being so subtly conveyed.

True beauty is inseparable from the eye and mind of its beholder. It is to be cherished for its own sake. It cannot be banked, bartered, or sold. It is not for possession, but for contemplation. It offers itself as a balm for the sensitive inner soul, and for a reflecting of its unspeakable harmony—resulting in a measure of order in a place of unrest that could not be reached in any other way. To a less sensitive soul, it may offer nothing at all.

Beauty can be found everywhere in the natural, free for the enjoying by anyone with finely tuned senses and a receptive mind. It is not exclusive to the fresh and the new. Glimmerings of past experiences cling to an old or weathered face, a gnarled tree, or a fallen leaf. Our appreciation of antiques is due to the richness of an accumulation of happenings in time. The patina of age adds a dimension and a depth of interest that cannot be contrived or manufactured.

An object of the most intense beauty or extreme exquisiteness is to the Japanese *shibui.* No other word in any language quite captures the subtle blending of subjective elements that vibrates in that single one. Translated literally, it means "puckery" or "astringent," as in a slightly acid fruit such as the persimmon or grapefruit. But that hardly begins to approximate the restraint with many nuances that every Japanese understands to be *shibusa.*

> The world abounds with different aspects of beauty. The lovely, the powerful, the gay, the smart—all belong to the beautiful. Each person, according to his disposition and environment, will feel a special affinity to one or another aspect. But when his taste grows more refined, he will necessarily arrive at a beauty which is SHIBUI. Many a term serves to denote the secret of beauty, but this is the final word.
>
> Dr. Soctsu Yanagi

In a shibui way of thinking, the space contained within a teacup, the after-reverberation of a bell, and the untouched areas of a painting become important and imbued with subtle meaning. Serenity, silence, and tranquility pervade shibui expression. But there is nothing pretentious or exclusive about it. It has to do with normality and naturalness, and it is quite at home among the commonplace and ordinary. The Japanese folk crafts exhibit sensitive examples of it. Coarse texture and roughness are deeply appreciated, and are seen as the human stepping aside, allowing nature to come to the fore. The wood texture in a print, a rough, natural streak in a piece of glazed pottery, or even cracks, bubbles, or distortions that have occurred naturally in the firing are greatly prized as being particularly shibui.

In this dual world of relativities, absolute truth is no easier to realize than absolute beauty. But as long as we remain transient and ever-changing beings in an ever-changing experience, our compulsive striving toward an unattainable goal may be necessary to provide space and energy for playing out the endless living melody. The Japanese are realistically aware that, as material forms, they and their objects have a beginning and end. But they recognize the essential truth of either to be the continuity of change, in and out of expression, and not the unreality of a frozen moment in indivisible time.

For at least ten centuries, the people of Japan have been developing and practicing their finely attuned connoisseurship of graceful living. As far back as the Hein period (794-1392), their upper classes were conversing in poetry. Everything from food to manners to dress revolved around the principles of beauty. Music was universally accepted, as essential for daily living as food and drink.

The West's obsession with machines designed to work has left its people with a vague feeling that perfection must be beautiful, or that the beautiful must be perfect. Referring back to nature as the infallible master, one can easily see that perfection never was its intent, but normality and naturalness. Trees and flowers come in every degree of perfection, but hardly ever meet the ideal in every respect. Nonetheless, the overall impression is one of rightness and beauty. A slick, machinemade object may present a "perfect" appearance, but it is superficial and easy to read. It reveals its entire self at a glance, becoming tiresome and uninteresting as soon as the novelty wears away.

The normal and natural invites and intrigues. Nothing satisfies the attentive eye quite so much as the poetic melancholy of a blend of shibui qualities—a silvery weathered branch, rain on the garden rocks, moss on the north side of a tree,—and of course the many works of sensitive artists on the same level of expression.

Shibusa is not limited to objects of nature or art. The feeling can extend indefinitely to include almost any area of experience. The manner, style of living, of dress, or even the entire pattern of a life can sometimes be recognized as having reached that highest state of refinement and beauty. There are places that resonate with a magic beyond the range of reason. There are moments that shimmer with a kind of other worldly radiance. There are even those few rare people who seem to have integrated the shibui principles into every aspect of their being and doing. Those are the places, events, and people who linger with lasting significance, long after any tangible trace of them has passed.

8
Authorized Truth

The night sky and I are old friends. For a long time I have lived close to a vast, sandy beach where sky and water merge, and the line of sight stretches to infinity in a satisfyingly wide sweep of the eye.

Of course, I am fond of the day sky. I delight in the ever-changing spectrum of tints from palest violet through the varying intensities of blue to watermelon pink or flaming poppy. I revel in the sun filtering through sheets of silver fog or fair-weather clouds or blazing down on the sand, blistering the sun-bathers. I share the day sky with a lot of others. I see them scrutinizing it for signs of a weather change. It determines their activities and, for a lot of them, even their states of mind.

The night sky is altogether different—less public. In most places, it is blocked from general view by trees, roofs, and canopies, or lost in the glare of city lights. But the beach that I know so well shares a special relationship with the night sky. Out there, the heavens are still, mysterious, and incredibly boundless. My fascination has drawn me out regularly for more years than I care to count.

I know the patterns of the stars. I follow the phases of the moon. I feel wonder at the steady glow of the Milky Way. I note the flicker of each tiny star reaching my observing eye countless light years after the time it began. I watch for the occasional shooting star, or the added thrill of a shower of them streaking across my field of vision in stunning, silent beauty. I know well the difference between all of them and the tiny, artificial lights blinking from the small, fragile planes plying their way in and out of the local airport some miles distant. I can instantly spot the purposeful gleam of a jet arriving from some faraway land beyond the horizon. I am an experienced and dedicated observer of long standing, with a sharp eye and a keen interest. I would be less likely than most to misinterpret what I see in the night sky.

Nonetheless, one experience lingers in my memory, unexplained and, even yet, strangely bothersome—one that I hesitate to mention to anyone, or even think about too seriously myself. Yet, I am no less sure of it than I am of the existence of the bus that thundered down the street past me just this morning.

It was a clear night, one that would have appeared to the casual glance much the same as any other. I walked slowly, scanning the familiar sky with relaxed pleasure, my mind free-floating in the peace it had come to depend on following a hectic day in the human world.

Then, suddenly, my eye caught and held a

most amazing sight. I froze to instant attention. What I was seeing happened almost faster than I could comprehend. A large, perfectly round, pearl-white, luminous object streaked across the sky, appearing and disappearing almost within the blink of an eye. From where I was standing, it looked larger to me that the almost-full moon, and considerably closer to Earth. I felt stunned with a sense of having lost touch with my own reality—the startled participant in a waking dream.

Back at the house, I called a local amateur astronomer, known to most of his tongue-in-cheek neighbors as "that UFO nut." He told me that mine was the fourth call he had received that evening, all reporting essentially the same thing. He asked if the object had displayed any erratic behavior—backing up, gaining or losing altitude, or some such thing. It had not, I replied. It had sped a straight and silent path across the sky. In that case, he said, it must be assumed I had seen a "natural" phenomenon. That was that. I never heard it mentioned again. I rarely mention it myself. When I do, I find myself doubting the truth of what I am saying almost as much as does my patiently courteous listener.

Whatever it was that I saw did not seem readily identifiable or easily categorized within the structure of reality subscribed to by my time and culture. It is more comfortable, even for me, to pretend that I did not see what I did. By offering my experience to others I am, in effect, offering a monkey wrench to throw into the works of their truth system. Little wonder they laugh nervously, smile condescendingly, or back away and eye me with suspicion.

The lone maverick who sees and seeks a truth too different from the prevailing one of his time and culture is misunderstood, regarded with mistrust, even anger and aggression—or simply declared mad. Jesus was crucified for straying too far beyond the bounds of the acceptable thought of his time. In 1600 Giordana Bruno, after eight years of trial, was sent to the stake and burned as a magician for declaring that the universe was infinite and contained countless planets like the Earth. Galileo spent the last years of his life under house arrest for daring to postulate ideas incompatible with the Scriptures, which he refused to recognize as a scientific text. Even in this "land of the free," as late as the seventeenth century, the "witches" of Salem, Massachusetts, were mobbed and burned because they were suspected of dealing in areas of unauthorized truth.

However, since we humans also happen to be learning and evolving beings, it is inevitable that even an authorized truth will undergo gradual but steady alteration and change through time, expanding more or less beyond the old boundaries or, circumstances being just right, even pioneering in directions or dimensions theretofore not known to exist.

Before the twelfth century, in Europe the universe was regarded in a relatively passive and unquestioning way. While ready to acknowledge its unmistakable majesty and mystery, most felt there was little anyone could do to alter or control it. The Earth, transient and ever-changing, likewise was there to be accepted and dealt with in the best way one could—with all due respect, of course, since obviously one's life depended on it. But it was to the sky that those early people looked—to wonder and marvel at the eternal perfection of God's plan. It was in astrology that their minds and imaginations took airy flight, adding a dimension of fantasy and hope to their often uninspiring and difficult lives.

A significant shift from that point of view came when the European intellectuals familiarized themselves with Greek and Arab science and Aristotle's logical system of thought. It was tantalizing to those group-minded people to imagine that an individual experience might have value and importance in the context of the whole. The idea caught and held. Before long, universities began to appear, committed to teaching the radical new ideas. Young students flocked eagerly to them. They emerged confident, rational, and forward thinking, trained in questioning and investigative thought. A dialogue was beginning between man and his universe, in terms more equal than ever before.

A century later, another important shift occurred when Aristotle's hierarchical universe, created and arranged by the hand of God, met its first serious challenge. Toscanelli, an Italian proponent of the Arab thought, brought perspective geometry to the humanist thinkers of the early Renaissance, and with it came the tools of measurement. Everything, according to the new view, was measurable, and all could be related to a common standard. Balance and harmony were seen to be the essential elements of perfection. Architecture took a giant step forward. The mysterious earth suddenly seemed to offer itself invitingly in more intimate ways than ever before.

Johannes Gutenberg, with his printing press in the middle of the fifteenth century, introduced other exciting new possibilities to what had until then been an essentially oral society. Taking over the laborious task of the few lonely monks copying their manuscripts, the press promised to stretch the bounds of knowledge wide enough to include the common man. Little could they have dreamed of the communication revolution that was to evolve from that first tentative, small step.

Of all the major mind shifts in Western thought, probably Darwin's *Origin of the Species* caused the greatest stir and controversy. That modest book, packed with its bold affronts to conventional thought, thrust itself on a public where the biblical interpretation of world history held full and unchallenged sway. The six-day creation was unquestioned—a spiritually revealed fact. The Garden of Eden was looked upon as an equally infallible setting for the beginnings of humanity. And no one would have thought (or dared) to question the Church's 6000-year estimate of the Earth's age.

Darwin's appalling declaration of the Earth as a dynamic and evolutionary planet shocked the populace. That it might be possible for different kinds of organisms to evolve from a common ancestor, if given enough time, was a radical idea far beyond the mind-stretch of the average citizen. The Church bristled to defend its theological views, seen to be under enemy fire. Many others, who had been secure in the belief of themselves as fashioned exclusively in the image of God, felt threatened and angry to see humans demoted to the level of beasts—or so it seemed to them.

Undeniable geological evidence now stands firm in its revelation of an Earth billions of years older than the Scriptures would imply. The steady emergence of fossils, fitting together like the pieces of a long-lost puzzle, confirm much of what Darwin had to say. Evolution, to one degree or another, is all but universally accepted. Most of the controversy has quieted down—but not all. Heated echoes of dissent and denial still ring from behind the scenes even in today's atomic-age classrooms. Inexperienced youngsters are left to grapple with the big question by themselves, supplied with confusing, conflicting scientific and biblical views—and with no sensible instructor, who values his or her job, willing to take a definite stand on either.

Science has made a steady climb upward since its acceptance as the preferred route to an unbiased truth. Creative imaginations within it have astonished an admiring public with innovative extensions of the senses, allowing a far wider range of human awareness than would otherwise be possible. The telescope, microscope, and other instruments, as well as the revolutionary developments in locomotion and communication, have extended human capabilities far beyond what is "natural." Still, the differences brought about by these inventions, dramatic as they are, are in degree only and not in kind. What is happening now in quantum physics (and to some related degree in the other sciences) promises something more, whereby the very definition of reality enters a new realm of meaning.

Always, together with every change in world view, there comes a change in the dreams and expectations of those who embrace it. Scientists make discoveries that they can, first of all, envision in their imaginations. But the way they perceive the world around them determines the kind and quality of those visions and, subsequently, their material expressions. A style of living is created, keyed to that aspect of reality on which the popular belief is focused.

No interpretation of reality will ever be the ultimate or final one, beyond which truth-seekers of the future cannot go. Knowledge knows no bounds. Each revelation, even the newest, opens out in time to ever more exciting new vistas, endlessly inviting exploration and discovery. To suggest that "everything" of science, or any other field of learning, could ever be known is an error of the human ego. Reality is an infinitely faceted gem. Which beam of light strikes any particular eye depends on where the eye is and when. Seeing the whole truth revealed at any one time and in any one place would require the kind of omnipotence attributable only to God.

It is the way of us humans to cherish our own particular beam of truth as the right one, regarding all others, if not wrong then, certainly, less right than ours. Even within the same culture and era some, often with the very best of intentions, set about hoping to erase those lesser, or even "evil," truths of others, and to replace them with their own. One who sees differently is not seeing correctly.

Whatever "truth" happens to be the prevailing and accepted one on this earth can only be, at best, a minutely partial and totally relative one. Radio telescopes reach out hundreds of billions of light years into the vastness of space, receiving information directly from deep in the past. Yet all of it is only a small sampling of a tiny fraction of the totality to which we belong.

A human life is but the merest blip in cosmological time, and the entire history of our species is hardly more. Whatever small "truth" can be gained by us is inexorably slipping away with every second that contains, yet exceeds, the one before it—and the complexity keeps growing.

We are all part of a system—of a system—of a system, and so on and on. Family, school, community, country, planet. Our connections extend even into the universe beyond. The planet is part of its solar system. The solar system is part of its galaxy. The galaxy is part of its cluster. The cluster of galaxies joins others of its kind to create the "bubbly" pattern of the fabric of space-time. The ''bubbles'' are immense spherical shells of galaxies, surrounding and enclosing gigantic and mysterious voids, seemingly, containing no matter at all. The texture of space appears to be distinctly sponge-like.

Based on the scale of full reality (or at least as it is accessible to our scientific methods of observation), it seems recklessly bold to award the honor of front-running pioneers of reason and intelligence to one tiny Earth species. More likely (and a whole lot more modestly), conscious awareness appears naturally as soon as a suitable instrument for its support and conversion has been designed and perfected, allowing one tiny spark of the all-pervading light to glow into space-time—for a *very* short duration, and probably not the first, the only, or the brightest spark so far. Whenever matter reaches a certain critical stage of organization and development, those higher, more refined and involved qualities probably unfold—just as do the daisy's petals once the forces of nature have sufficiently evolved the idea potential in the seed.

Life may be only one of a multitude of expressions inherent in the cosmic purpose, each one equally necessary to the whole, and satisfying to whatever has been chosen to express it. Then again, intelligent life may be the one underlying reality—the first cause and the last effect.

There is no need for humans to suffer any feelings of inadequacy due to their size or temporality. They ought not to feel in the slightest elbowed aside, or mere observers from the edge of things. They are superbly designed for the niche that was there for them to fill. They are as involved with the whole as anything else and, probably, just as important to its overall functioning and purpose (in a universal sense).

The puddle reflects the sky without pride or humility. The microcosm reflects the macrocosm. In some miraculous way, the inner joins the outer, with no known bounds separating either one. The longest journey begins at one's own front door, and ends at one's own back door. Astronauts, who have ventured a mere step from their home planet, have returned impressed, not so much by the grandeur of what they have seen as by the changes they sense to have occurred in themselves.

The vast collection of wisdom accumulated through time from the inner resources of our most worthy ancestors, if it were to be combined, compared, and properly understood, would probably be more than enough for planet Earth to hold its own in any company. But too much of our valuable heritage has been scattered, hoarded, wrongly interpreted, rejected, or forgotten.

The trouble was that until only recently most of our official truth-gatherers chose to confine themselves, each in his or her own little cell or laboratory, declining to combine efforts or share views with any but another of similar bent. As a consequence, science and philosophy, as well as almost every other discipline of learning, kept to itself, jealously guarding its "purity" with passionate single-mindedness. Now, all that is beginning to change. New methods of communicating and comparing ideas, with a speed and ease never before dreamed of, are setting the darkest pockets of the Earth aglow with an interchange of understanding between neighbors of the farthest reaches. Truth-seekers of every field, every continent, every country can no longer avoid rubbing shoulders in expounding their frequently parallel views. The latest word is refreshing, and the newly emerging ''truth'' is finding definition in terms as multidimensional as the universe itself.

In a universe as vast and incomprehensible as this one, individual meaning can come only through connectedness. Parts are strictly neutral, mere ciphers in themselves. The worth is in the living connections between them. It is the melody not the notes wherein the meaning lies.

9
The Language of the Birds

The "language of the birds" is referred to in a number of old legends belonging to several ancient traditions. Understanding the language was thought to come through participation in high initiations, or as the hard won reward for a "slaying of the dragon." The dragon, in old symbolism, traditionally held guard over the priceless treasure of immortality, usually metaphorically represented by some object. Slaying the dragon meant a conquest of the prize which, in turn, implied integration at the center. The center was the silent point at which communication with the very highest states of being became possible.

In ancient texts, birds and angels were symbols referring to high states of consciousness. The "word," whether of angels, birds, or God, dispatched from those high states, acted as a knock upon the silence to be answered by the music of a soul.

Traditionally, holy books, hymns, and mantras were written in rhythmic verse to be chanted or read, the resulting vibrations felt to aid one in approaching that high level. The rhythmic sound, quite as much as the content of the word, was thought to be a medium for evoking a high emotional response. Music, with its potential for complicated patterns of rhythm, was favored as a particularly accommodating art in evoking touches with the spirit. The dedicated composer, by lending his finely tuned inner ear to intensive development and experience, might in time be able to translate the harmony that he "heard." If the performing artist proved to be equally sensitive and responsive, he too might be able to stand aside at the peak of his inspiration, and allow the theme to pass through him almost unobstructed.

Ludwig van Beethoven, the great musical genius of the late eighteenth and early nineteenth centuries, left behind him a legacy of music that is considered to be among the world's most inspired. The last of his compositions might be regarded as being particularly accurate translations of the "language of the birds."

It has been said that this composer used his music to ascend the graduated scale of his own levels of consciousness. He began with a natural aptitude, great powers of concentration, and a firm understanding of the basics of music. He journeyed on from there to the highest realms of his spiritual self. The developmental steps of that extraordinary man of music, whose sensitive inner ear "heard" the sounds of some great reality beyond the capabilities of most others, illustrates in a particularly vivid way the gradation of possible human levels, as they rise to the soaring heights of subjectivity or spirituality.

In following Beethoven's music as a reflection of his spiritual development, it is important to consider the man who was to set musical standards of excellence for centuries to come, as apart from the all-too-human one who struggled through a lifetime of personal tragedies and defeats, culminating in the most cruel blow of all—his eventual deafness. But, as history so frequently reminds us, a powerful drive concentrated in some special ability can seize the life of an artist and bend it mercilessly to its own voracious will. Sometimes, as in the case of Beethoven, it can extort such a heavy expenditure in one direction that there is a destructive draining from another.

Ludwig van Beethoven entered the world of music as a precocious twelve year old. His first three sonatas, composed in those early years, remained unpublished and caused no particular stir. Instead, they happened to fit in rather unremarkably with the prevailing classical modes of his time.

By the time Beethoven had reached the age of twenty-four, he was intensely involved with music. He was already well on his way, being noticed by the critics as an especially promising young composer. His works produced during those years met expectations as the work of a major talent. However, there was still no hint of the unprecedented genius of the man, or the extraordinary masterpieces that were yet to come. In this, Beethoven's "mature ego" stage, his works were still mostly self-involved—inspired and patterned after his own moods and emotions.

He took a giant step forward for both himself and all music with the composition of his Third Symphony, the *Eroica*. Unlike those earlier pieces consisting of a series of personal moods, this one exceeded the bounds of convention. It attempted that which had never been attempted before. *Eroica* was a complex arrangement of interrelated and interwoven ideas and concepts, blended together into a kind of organic unity that was totally new in the experience of music.

Response to the *Eroica* by its first audience was electrifying. Marek (1969) wrote:

> Hearing the *Eroica* for the first time must have been an experience similar to that of hearing news of the splitting of the atom. To some it was maddening, to others it was frightening. To others—altogether thrilling. Those who knew music well must have perceived the discovery of a new galaxy of music.

Unfortunately, the impact of Beethoven's remarkable achievement was tempered by his oncoming deafness, then beginning its slow and steady advance, threatening seriously to jeopardize his continuing involvement in the world of music. But the momentum of that supremely dedicated musician's inspiration drove him on and, despite the magnitude of his handicap, his work continued to prosper.

It was not until his final works—the Ninth Symphony, the *Missa Solemnis,* and his last three piano sonatas—that Beethoven himself was finally satisfied that he understood the art of composing. He reported reaching so near to the

Godhead that he experienced music timelessly—all at once. He declared that the music he had the power to write down was mere "riff-raff" compared to that which he intimately knew. His music, at that stage, was not being written around any particular form or theme constructed to carry the thought. Instead, it was more nearly that of the thought itself. "It has that serenity which...passes beyond beauty...The virginal purity of this music...suggests...spirit not yet made flesh" (Sullivan, 1964).

Near the end, Beethoven was obliged to use an ear trumpet to pick up the fragments of sound that increasingly evaded him. Eventually, he was unable to hear a single note of the performances of some of his most inspired and inspiring work. Nonetheless, his last compositions reflected difficulties transcended, and a soul at last released to peace and freedom.

Ludwig van Beethoven, relieved of his earthly struggles, left a final promise:

> No evil fate shall touch my music. He who divines its secret is freed from the unhappiness that haunts the whole world of man.
>
> Cited in *Keys,* 1971

That an individual has the potential to reach higher levels of consciousness than those normally experienced is not a new idea. Religions of all cultures, all times, have been unanimous in their recognition of those high flights of the spirit, and most devised their own methods of aspiring toward them.

Psychologists of the West have been less inclined to admit to any stage of psychological development beyond the well established "adult-ego," and most are even likely to pass off what might seem to be clear evidence to the contrary as pathological, probably requiring diagnosis and treatment. But a particularly high level of consciousness has long been recognized and variously described by less earthbound thinkers as "cosmic consciousness," the Eastern "Brahmic Splendor," or, in the words of Walt Whitman who had a lot to say on the subject, ". . .the ineffable light. . .light, rare, untellable, lighting the very light. . .beyond all signs, descriptions, and languages." In India, someone who has achieved such a high state is called *jivamukti* (*Jiva*-soul; *mukti*-liberated or enlightened), and thought to be someone in direct touch with what in the West has been called the "sacred unconscious"—or final substrate that opens out to the universe as it actually is, one and whole.

Modern science acknowledges a hierarchy of units in the order of nature. It sees evolution as the process of unfolding higher systems, each one more complex, organized, and inclusive than the one before. And since the human mentality is an expression of that same nature, the idea of transcending one level and emerging on the next would seem to correspond with the natural pattern of growth. There seems to be no reason why humanity should not transcend itself, just as it lifted itself into another level beyond the animal state. But before a decisive elevation in the development of humanity as a whole could occur, it would seem that the change must first be realized in a few—then subsequently in an increasingly greater number of individuals.

We do not need to search far for examples of those who seem to have lived well beyond the normal level of being. Scattered throughout time, a handful of mystic sages, as well as exceptionally gifted performers and thinkers in every field, have left their indelible marks on the pages of history. Clearly Christ, Buddha, Socrates, Lao Tse, Leonardo da Vinci, as well as Beethoven and many others both recognized and unrecognized, exceeded the standards expected of ordinary humans—at least, in one particular aspect of their lives.

Even with these extraordinary achievers in mind, it would be impossible for us, in our present stage, to foresee such a revolutionary change in our species with any degree of clarity. Every step of evolutionary advance enfolds within itself all preceding stages, but opens the way for new possibilities that would be unimaginable to any of an earlier expression.

Fossil remains reveal something of the character of evolution. It appears there may be long periods of stability, followed by sudden, dramatic bursts of change. Thus, it seems reasonable to predict that any evolution beyond the human level would not produce a mere "superman," but a being of quite another kind—a distinctly new order of life.

It would seem that some early signs revealed in great characters might point in the direction to which an evolutionary advance is inclining, or in looking back we might see traces of ourselves in a stage below. We sometimes see the brief glimmer of human traits in the higher animals. There are sudden, startling bursts of mutual understanding, as qualities we ordinarily assume to be exclusively our own blink through a partially opened animal innocence, before the dividing veil between species drops once again.

Similar clues indicating where the human may be heading into the future could be there, too, for the looking. It might be relevant that even our earliest and most primitive human ancestors seemed irresistibly drawn toward the values expressed in religions, music, and the rest of the arts. The yearning toward some impossibly high goal has kept the human race exerting effort to reach it against all odds, even when the goal, itself, seemed obscure and unattainable. Those ardently sought values appear to be free of our major human limitations of time and space—a fact that accounts for the difficulty an ordinary human has in getting as firm a grip on any of them as he or she might like.

One can only guess what life as an enlightened being within an enlightened humanity might be. In imagining it, sentimentality is the greatest danger. Evolution is firm and tough. Thus far, it has avoided sentimentality, and it is not likely to veer very far from its natural course. Living involves responsibilities and tasks to be done—hard tasks. No one should expect that scenario to change very much.

An adept of the new consciousness would

probably not be one who meditated his time away on some mountain top. More likely, his involvement would be a full dedication to the world, with a heightened refinement of understanding and purpose. A ''cleansed perception'' would probably not reveal the infinite as an unapproachable, personified absolute of power. More likely, it would be seen as constituting the reality of whatever was at hand—a view with which the adept could readily identify, since he would be conscious of sharing the same universal spirit that was the essence of his own being.

To hope that humanity could ever reach the condition of total harmony and holistic identification is probably being overly optimistic. Still, this may well be the direction in which we are slowly advancing. Some hard facts of science are already chipping away at the long-standing illusion of a world of ''things,'' and revealing, in its stead, a web of connections that bears no division—even between the least of them. A climate favorable to a change in human consciousness is being prepared. If individual greed and irresponsibility do not prove to be our downfall, then the change may come to our descendents in its own good time.

In the past, growth into new and higher levels has always been characterized by a simplification of facts, and a unification of relations. Changes now in the making still hold to those basics, but with a difference. This time, human limitations are being overstepped, as each mind joins to countless others in a vast network of communication. Thought is connecting with thought to create a consciousness that exceeds any individual, and yet promises to include each in a more aware and fulfilling experience than has ever before been possible.

Perhaps the fresh, new kindergartners—frowning over their kiddie-computers, learning to trust and cooperate with the perceptions and interpretations of an intelligence so much broader than their own—will become the front-runners of the new humanity, perhaps a humanity in which cosmic consciousness will have become the realistic goal for everyone.

A mind of cosmic consciousness would still be far from ultimate awareness. Just as young children, attaining to their level of self-consciousness, do not know everything about themselves, neither would one know all there was to know of the cosmos simply by becoming conscious of it. However, it would mean the experiencing of reality in an altogether new way—as intuitive and holistic, more unified than separative, more subjective than objective, and more spiritual than material.

Ludwig van Beethoven died at the early age of fifty-six. Yet it appears that, in least one aspect of his life, he far exceeded the reach of his peers. It has been suggested that the immense worldly suffering he was fated to endure may have accelerated his development beyond its normal rate.

''Movement by reason of resistance, produces a combination that is life,'' said Honoré de Balzac. The way of psychological or spiritual growth does not seem to be the way of comfort and ease. The paths of great achievers have, more often than not, been uncommonly rocky ones. Those few most likely to qualify as the twentieth century's transcendent souls—Mother Teresa, Gandhi, Albert Schweitzer, and others—have almost invariably chosen lives of struggle and hardship in which to pursue their lofty goals.

The high priority we Westerners give to making things ever easier may not be doing ourselves the service we intend. Muscles need firm and steady resistance if they are to develop and grow strong. It seems not unlikely that our subjective natures may require equally rigorous training and testing if they are to reach their full potential. We could be retarding or, possibly, even destroying our opportunity for moving on to a higher level by creating conditions in which so many of us remain unchallenged and psychologically and spiritually flabby.

The secrets of our material universe would never have been sought and so painstakingly gathered, nor would the masterpieces have been conceived and created, if there had been no dragons to slay—and if there had been no individuals of vision who, against all possible odds, had mustered the strength, perseverence, and courage to put their lives on the line in slaying them.

Is a full and balancing development in the subjective dimension of our human natures—at least equally as complex and powerful as the objective—likely to require any less?

10
Stir a Flower and Trouble a Star

It is now May in this small, seaside community where I live. Spring is hosting a carnival of conscious and unconscious creativity. Nature proliferates into every new form possible to this particular environment. In addition, there are bursts of human energy devoted to new creations. Everywhere people are planting gardens, building boats and houses, or absorbing themselves with paints, brushes, and a propped easel.

Every spring is unique, not just a rerun of the one before. Each is vibrant and alive with countless new changes and adaptations, most too small or slow to be noticed by anyone. This is not just another spring but, if left to itself without any interference, it would be more refined and complex than the one preceding it.

Seagulls are circling out from the islands, flocking over the fishermen's boats, scavenging for their ravenous, newly hatched young. There is a white swan nesting beside the pond this year. Red-winged blackbirds challenge me when I walk too close to their nesting mates. I see round, moist-eyed rabbits with translucent pink ears, out for a first shy look at the world. Fiddlehead ferns unfurl in shady places, and dandelions light up the dingy corners. Life, in multiplying, is intensifying those qualities most essential to its continuance and development, phasing out some and adding others.

All seems deceptively quiet and peaceful in my back yard and, probably, in yours. But the gentle, pastoral scene that stirs the blood of the spring poet would present an altogether different picture if time could be accelerated to include the whole of it within the infinitesimal scale of a human lifetime. Our own petty attempts at manufactured violence lighting the TV and movie screens would pale next to what is going on naturally and continuously in every square inch of the globe (and beyond), and mostly without our awareness or concern.

Every day, all day, there are species sparring for position in their life-and-death struggles for survival. On every side, life is forcing its way into being, battling to satisfy its voracious needs, crowding out or devouring the old and the weak. Forces of the Yins and Yangs are squaring off, compromising their oppositions in the best way that they can, balancing against the collapse of the system that is dependent upon their upholding it.

Even the earth, "solid as the ground under your feet," has evolved to its present, relative stability through an incredibly violent history of upheavals and transformations. And it still goes on. Boiling water and mud bubble up from some unseen, underground inferno; volcanoes erupt under the sea; continents still shift, raising mountains, wrinkling and splitting the crust of the earth, and nudging the land masses hither and yon. Even the Grand Canyon, majestic symbol of peace and tranquility (or so it would seem), is estimated to have been undersea at least seven times since the birth of the planet.

Now quite suddenly (or so it may appear), one species has risen above the others, flowering into a new kind of curiosity, imagination, and above all with the ability to step back, measure, and evaluate a little of what is going on, even realizing itself as inseparable from the events it proposes to study, and understanding that simply through its attention it will, somehow, alter everything.

The most disturbing revelation that strikes critical observers is that the species to which they, themselves, belong is in serious trouble. Though the survival of such fragile and physically defenseless creatures has been challenged countless times before, this threat is of another kind. Not only are the scope, the intensity, and seeming irreversibility more formidable than ever before, but this time if the experiment that is the species itself should fail, it would not be due to a slip in the mechanics of nature, but to a tragedy of its own making—not a natural death, but an evolutionary suicide.

Some, like Sydney Harris, believe that we are a failed experiment and near the beginning of the end. A syndicated columnist, he writes his article "A Failed Experiment" in the very same issue of the newspaper which, on another page, briefly notes the fact of his death.

> We seem doomed to exterminate ourselves as a species, through hate or greed, accident or insanity, as a temporal failure in the cosmic laboratory. . . . The Creator, in my view, is neither infinitely wise nor infinitely powerful, but infinitely patient and infinitely ingenious . . . . She/He will start all over again, from the neutron, and then the amoeba, fabricating life upwards to intelligence once more, and with each try, getting closer to the pattern held in the Divine Mind. . . . All religions have childish names for God, because we are still a childish species, vain enough to covet personal immortality, and yearning for assurances that are beyond the power of the Great Experimenter.

Others see cause for optimism, interpreting the confusion of direction and values in today's world as a prelude to transformation—the struggle of a butterfly about to emerge from its chrysalis, a new creature.

The state in which modern man find himself is one of dangerous imbalance due to at least a century's narrow concentration on one aspect of the mind's ability, to the neglect and progressive degeneration of another—the Yang to the near exclusion of the Yin. Through an unprecedented burst of technological breakthroughs, immense power for good and evil now rests in the hands of Western man, including areas heretofore ascribed only to the discretion of God. The race is on to match those awesome technological skills and tools with correspondingly high levels of psychological and spiritual development, to ensure that they do not get out of hand and pave the way to humanity's own destruction.

Events over the past few decades have fostered some cautious hope in the growing exchange of respect. There is a new recognition of common, holistic goals between the traditionally antagonistic disciplines of spirituality (as distinct from "religiosity," and narrowly interpreted dogma) and science.

The new paradigm of complementarity easing in to replace the old conflict has brought unifying influences that soften the tone of separateness, creating bridges of understanding between the East and the West, the ancient and modern, and even within the sciences themselves.

Latest word from the physicists is that Einstein's unfulfilled dream of discovering an underlying principle that would unite all known forces of the universe into one has possibly been realized in the new superstring theory. Einstein, with his theory of relativity, established himself as unqualified master in understanding the secrets of energy, gravity, and space-time. But quantum mechanics, having to do with matter, was not in his direct line of interest, and he failed to realize that the key to the unity that he sought might be found in a combination of the principles of relativity and quantum mechanics. In the 1930s Paul Dirac combined the two ideas that are the cornerstone of modern physics—relativity and quantum mechanics.

The superstring theory does away with particles as the building blocks of matter, once and for all. It postulates, instead, that all matter, including our own bodies as well as everything else of substance, is ultimately composed of tiny, vibrating "strings." The "music" created by these vibrating strings is that which we ordinarily experience as actual matter. The unity between the different vibrating frequencies is the same that unites all the musical tones and rules of harmonics within the concept of a violin string. In short, the superstring theory is believed to combine the diversity of all frequencies in the universe into the harmony of just one "symphony"—or a single mathematical equation.

The "strings" are not ever likely to make it to the TV screen for public viewing. They are far too small to be observed by even the most sensitive of our instruments—estimated, as they are, to be about one hundred billion billion times smaller than a proton. The protons and neutrons of every atom are, themselves, basically made up of these same tiny strings.

Something of the chill of materialism warms to a theory like that. Perhaps the poets, in their preoccupation with symmetry and rhythm, have been more "scientific" all along than even they have imagined. Seeing ourselves as "composed" of frequencies rather than "built" of particles ought to make a difference in one's self-esteem—and, correspondingly, in one's view of others.

And then there is light! We are told that, as material bodies, we have the theoretical potential to manifest as light (radiation or energy) as an alternative to the earthbound masses that we see ourselves to be. Einstein assured us of that possibility with his famous equation. $E=mc^2$. Not that transforming to a beam of ethereal light is within anyone's range of personal option as yet, but it is nice to know that the possibility exists.

Antimatter (negatively charged) is just one phenomenon among many in the dazzling new spectrum of possibilities permitted by the new physics. Its existence, unlike some of the others, has passed beyond the stage of speculation into demonstrable fact. Antimatter might be described as a "mirror-image" of the kind of matter that makes up our earth. The interesting thing about it (or frightening, depending on how great one speculates his chances to be of meeting up with some of it) is that matter and antimatter are known to harbor an unshakable and permanent grudge. In fact, were they ever to risk even the best-intentioned rendezvous, the result would be an instantaneous neutralization of them both, leaving behind only an explosion of energy, guaranteed to put any mere hydrogen bomb to shame. Shaking hands with a being from an antimatter world would be a mistake of the first order. Hopefully, there are not too many seeking contact, and if there should be, long distance communication will have to do.

Fortunately, the cost of creating an antimatter bomb appears to be prohibitive, and not likely to be considered as a replacement for the ones we already have (stocked in an obscenity of excess). But, even as I write, shades of other denouncements of deadly possibilities, turned askew by time and circumstance, pass before my uneasy mind. It is not reassuring to note that a bomb of antimatter would be nearly 100 percent efficient, as compared to the approximately 1 percent efficiency of the hydrogen bomb.

Other, equally bizarre stretches of the scientific imagination continue to light up thought horizons, as knowledge advances into the unseen and the abstract. A favorite theme of science fiction writers has long been the appearance of some strange being from another dimension. Now the superstring theory adds some credence to that fantasy by conceding the possibility of a ''sister'' universe of other dimensions. It is thought that it and our own may have been joined in just one ten-dimensional unit in the beginning—the ''Big Bang'' marking the time in which the original ''cracked'' and separated into two distinct universes. However, posits of such farflung speculation are quite clear about the ''sister'' universe's inaccessibility to us. They tell us that it may have shrunk to an incredibly small size—smaller than the nucleus of an atom, thus, positioning it far outside the possibility of earthly experience.

From all indications, that critical wrenching apart of the many-dimensional original easily rates as the undisputed spectacular of all time—so violent, in fact, that its echo is still to be heard as interference in radio antennae, and the best proof yet that the beginning was, indeed, a cataclysmic explosion.

Few theories, however, intrigue the scientists more than does the one of black holes, mysteriously and skillfully eluding straightforward detection, yet fulfilling all indirect expectations of their presence. A black hole is imagined to be a trumpet-like depression in the fabric of space-time, created by the gravitational collapse of a massive star. No escape is possible for anything, once ''sucked'' into the flared end of the trumpet. Not even light would be able to escape the intensity of its powerful gravitational forces.

No human imagination could picture a place like that in any kind of detail. But it has been suggested that the black hole might prove to be a ''gateway'' between two parallel universes—or even, if the stem of the trumpet were curved (as it may possibly be), it could be the pathway to another part of the same universe.

At this point, some restless reader might, understandably, ask: What does all this talk of a mind-reeling universe, superstrings, and black holes, all beyond my power to observe and experience, have to do with me? My days are confined within the hours of daylight, extending neither before nor after the brief span of a lifetime. My thoughts are preoccupied with paying the rent and keeping my family well, clothed, and fed. What difference if my body be one of particles or strings? It gets just as cold, as tired or hungry either way. It is born, lives, and dies—but the how, why, and where of it is mostly outside my consent or control.

And, just as understandably, the reply might be: It seems hardly any wonder that an individual might feel pressed into a meaningless existence, looking back at the depressingly bleak picture of humanity that Darwinians of the strictest order have been offering over the past several generations. It is not too personally uplifting to be told that one's self amounts to little more than a fluke in time, with no greater purpose or plan than a random tossing of the cosmic hat.

Hard-core evolutionists, for all those years, have been evasive in accounting for the nobler aspects of human nature. They have had remarkably little to say of the why and wherefore of music, literature, art, religion, and all those other fruits of the spirit that we instinctively feel to be our crowning achievements. Nor have they been able to explain satisfactorily the seemingly deliberate order and intelligent patterning inherent in the process of development, or the clever methods devised by nature to circumvent difficulties encountered in the paths of progress. Some would even have us believe that the entire cosmic creation, from which we humans have sprung like late-blooming daisies in a long-standing meadow, to be less creative, reasonable, and intelligent than even we small struggling creatures are.

How much more pride in being human, and how much more respect for one another would come with the feeling that each is inseparably included as part of an intelligent operation, secure within the harmony of a natural, unfolding pattern of purpose and meaning—rather than just a chance coming together of parts that fit. In such a view, there would have been no blind and mindless groping through time in search of an eye, or a brain. Instead, those instruments would be seen as ideas existing prior to the assembling of parts. Slow development does not necessarily mean lack of direction toward a desired result.

It seems reasonable to believe that intelligence came first. Nothing comes from nothingness. When anything is beyond the grasp of human understanding or sense, the mind invents a darkness or a zero. But there is an incalculable infinite hidden in the zero and, beyond the range of human senses, there is light within the darkness. Light is the common denominator. It does not belong exclusively to the suns. They are only physical concentrations of it. We, ourselves, are just as much of it and, in our better moments, glow with it. Enlightenment, when it comes, shines not to the seeker, but through him.

> Nature and ego and the personal being. . . do not make up the whole of existence. For existence is not merely a glorious or a vain, a wonderful or a dismal panorama of a constant mutation of becoming. There is something eternal, immutable, imperishable, a timeless self-existence that is not affected by the mutations of nature. . . always pure, complete, great and unwounded. . . . To become spirit, no longer merely a mind and ego, is the opening word of this message of liberation.
>
> Sri Aurobindo
> *Essays on the Gita*

Bibliography

Abraham, David. 1987. *The Perceptual Implications of Gaia. ReVision,* Vol. 9, No. 2, Winter/Spring, 1986.

Andrews, Donald Hatch.1966. *The Symphony of Life.* Unity Village, Mo.: Unity Books.

Aurobindo, Sri. 1966. *Essays on the Gita.* Pondicherry, India: Sri Aurobindo Press.

Bohm, David. 1980. *Wholeness and the Implicate Order.* London, Boston and Henley: Routledge & Kegan Paul.

Capra, Fritjof. *The Tao of Physics.* New York: Bantam.

Cole, K.C. 1985. *Sympathetic Vibrations.* New York: Bantam.

Combs, Allan L. *Synchronicity: A Synthesis of Western Theories and Eastern Perspectives. ReVision,* Vol. 5, No. 1, Spring 1982.

Davies, Paul. 1983. *God and the New Physics.* New York: Simon and Schuster, Inc.

Dickenson, Emily. 1960. *The Complete Poems of Emily Dickenson.* Thomas H. Johnson, ed. Boston: Little, Brown & Co.

Funk, Joel. 1982. *Beethoven, A Transpersonal Analysis. ReVision,* Vol. 9, No. 2, Winter/Spring 1986.

Hitchcock, John L. 1986. *Atoms, Snowflakes and God.* Wheaton, Ill.: Theosophical Pub. House.

Jung, C. G. 1973. *Synchronicity: An Acausal Connecting Principle.* First Princeton/Bollingen paperback ed. Princeton: Princeton University Press.

Keys, J. 1971. *Only Two Can Play This Game.* New York: Bantam.

Bibliography

Lovelock, J. E. 1979. *A New Look at Life on Earth.* Oxford: Oxford U. Press.

Marek, G. 1969. *Beethoven: Biography of a Genius.* New York: Funk & Wagnalls.

Nicoll, Maurice. 1984. *Living Time.* Boulder & London: Shambhala.

Pagels, Heinz R. 1983. *The Cosmic Code.* New York: Bantam.

Sheldrake, Rupert A. 1981. *A New Science of Life.* Los Angeles: Tarcher, Inc.

Talbot, Michael. 1981. *Mysticism and the New Physics.* New York: Bantam.

Thompson, Francis. *Works of Francis Thompson.* W. Meynell, ed. New York: AMS Press.

Von Weizsäcker, Carl Friedrich. 1980. *The Unity of Nature.* New York: Farrar, Straus, Giroux.

Walsh, Roger N., and Frances Vaughan, eds. 1980. *Beyond Ego.* Los Angeles: J. P. Tarcher, Inc.

Wilbur, K. 1980. *The Atman Project.* Wheaton, Ill.: Theosophical Pub. House.

Wood, Barry. 1970. *The Magnificent Frolic.* Philadelphia: Westminster Press.

Young, Louise B. 1986. *The Unfinished Universe.* New York: Simon and Schuster.

QUEST BOOKS
are published by
The Theosophical Society in America,
Wheaton, Illinois 60189-0270,
a branch of a world organization
dedicated to the promotion of brotherhood and
the encouragement of the study of religion,
philosophy, and science, to the end that man may
better understand himself and his place in
the universe. The Society stands for complete
freedom of individual search and belief.
In the Classics Series well-known
theosophical works are made
available in popular editions.